Favorite Northwest Flies

TYING & FISHING

By Steve Probasco

Probasco's Favorite Northwest FLIES

Steve Probasco

Frank Amato
PORTLAND

Acknowledgments

I would like to thank all those tiers who have shared fly patterns
with me over the years. A special thanks to the Griffin Company
for providing the fly-tying tools used in this book, and
Angler's Sport Group for providing
the Daiichi hooks.

Frank Amato Publications, Inc.
P.O. Box 82112, Portland, Oregon 97282
503·653·8108 • www.amatobooks.com

All photographs by the author unless otherwise noted.

Book & Cover Design: Kathy Johnson
Printed in Singapore
Softbound ISBN: 1-57188-144-1   UPC: 0-66066-00344-7
Hardbound ISBN: 1-57188-234-0   UPC: 0-66066-00488-8

1 3 5 7 9 10 8 6 4 2

Dedication

To my fishing partners who always bum flies from me.

Now you can tie your own!

Contents

Foreword

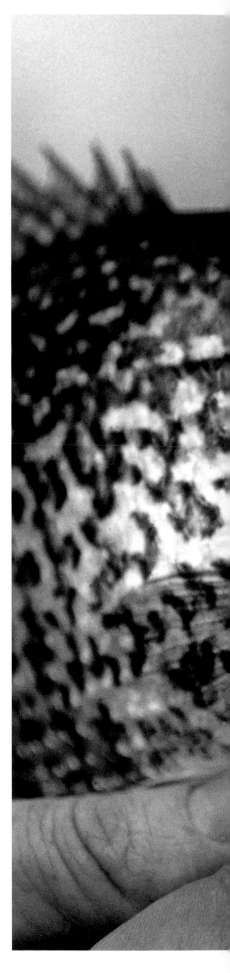

In 1986 I wrote a book titled *Fly Patterns for the Pacific Northwest*. At the time I couldn't help but wonder if there was really a need for another fly tying book. There were stacks of them on the market. But most of the books were about general fly tying—patterns for Western rivers, Eastern rivers, bass, saltwater species, etc. None delt specifically with the diverse fishing found in the Pacific Northwest—so I wrote the book. Within a couple years the book completely sold out. I guess it was a good idea.

Since that time, stacks more fly tying books have hit the market. And again, they cover everything under the sun...except flies for the Pacific Northwest. So, again, I found myself writing a book on Northwest fly patterns.

This book is not intended to be an all-inclusive pattern manual. Nor is it intended to cover all of the flies that are effective for Northwest fishing. What this book will do is cover the patterns that I personally use more than any others over the past several years. To select the flies for this book I looked through my fly boxes and pulled the patterns I most often go for. The flies found in these pages are patterns I use for trout, steelhead, salmon, bass, bottomfish, whitefish, shad, and carp.

I often sit at the tying bench and experiment with materials and fly designs. Rarely, with the exception of some of the time-proven standards, do I tie any given pattern the same way twice. For example; even on a standard like the Woolly Bugger, one day I may use chenille for the body, the next time I need Buggers I might use dubbing, the next time leech yarn. The same holds true with most flies—I use the materials at hand.

Many of the flies here are variations of standard patterns—versions that came about by the experimenting with different materials. Several of the fly patterns in this book are of my own design—flies that you can't buy anywhere. A few were designed by friends. Some I don't even know of their history.

I encourage you to experiment when tying flies. Experiment with materials, hooks and techniques. If you don't have the exact materials for any given pattern, substitute. Be creative. There are no rules here.

I am not going to take up space in this book talking about materials, tools, or techniques. You can find that information in nearly all of the other tying books on the market. I am assuming you are already adept at fly tying, and mostly interested in the fly patterns featured here because you thumbed through this book and a few flies caught your eye. But if not, the step-by-step photos and instruction on selected patterns should make the tying of any pattern in this book easy enough for those with even moderate tying skills.

I do, however, want to mention one thing about tying tools. Don't skimp when purchasing those basic tools, or your vise. Tying with quality equipment is a pleasure. Tying with cheap, poorly made tools is frustrating, and your finished flies will show it.

Trout

Trout are undoubtedly targeted with the fly more than any other Northwest species. The myriad lakes, rivers and streams found in Northwest waters where trout are found make this so. Whether it is floating a dry fly through a riffle in a mountain stream, or crawling a dragonfly nymph through the weeds in a desert lake, fly anglers across the Northwest seek out trout.

In this section I will cover some of my favorite patterns for Northwest trout. No, these are not the only patterns that work well, but they are the ones I reach for most often when I am on a trout chasing mission.

Parachute Adams

The Parachute Adams is to dry flies what the Pheasant Tail is to nymphs. Although you can find this pattern in several fly tying books, I simply had to include it here as it is the single most important general mayfly imitation there is.

When tied in a variety of sizes, the Adams covers several mayfly species as well as adult midges. Also, learning to tie this pattern will pave the way to tying a plethora of other parachute dry flies.

Hook: Daiichi 1180, size 6-24
Thread: Gray
Wing: Brown or white calf tail
Tail: Grizzly hackle fibers
Body: Gray dubbing
Hackle: 1 brown and 1 grizzly neck hackle

Step 1: Tie in the wing post as shown.

Step 2: Secure the hackles to the wing post.

Step 3: Tie in the tail.

Step 4: Dub on the body of gray dubbing tapering slightly larger towards the head of the fly.

Step 5: Wind the hackles together around the wing post 2 or 3 turns and secure.

Step 6: Finish head and cement to complete the Adams Parachute.

Elk Hair Caddis

One of the most popular adult caddisfly patterns is the Elk Hair Caddis. This fly is especially good in moving water. It floats well, casts a general caddisfly silhouette, and above all, fools plenty of trout. This is a must-have fly in every trout fisher's box.

Hook: Daiichi 1170 size 8-16
Thread: 6/0 (match body color)
Body: Fur or synthetic dubbing. Olives, browns, rust (colors of caddisflies vary. Take a selection of earth-tone colors)
Hackle: Brown neck, or match body color
Wing: Elk body hair

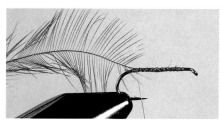

Step 1: Tie in a hackle by the tip.

Step 2: Twist dubbing material to your thread and wind on a body as shown.

Step 3: Wind hackle forward and secure.

Step 4: Tie in a small bunch of elk body hair as shown.

Step 5: Trim the elk hair into a head as pictured. Whip finish and cement to complete the Elk Hair Caddis.

Foam-Wing Caddis

This version of the adult caddis is one I came up with out of necessity. While fishing a small caddis hatch on a western river I was having problems keeping track of my small imitation among all the naturals. After returning home, I started experimenting and came up with the foam wing.

The foam wing makes the fly highly visible and also very buoyant. It is equally at home in moving and still waters.

Hook: Daiichi 1100, size 16-20
Thread: Match dubbing color
Body: Browns or olive dubbing (match naturals on the water)
Hackle: Neck to match body color
Wing: Fly foam cut to shape

Tying Steps
Step 1: Tie in a quality neck hackle by the tip at the bend of the hook.
Step 2: Wind on a body of dubbing and palmer the hackle forward.
Step 3: Cut a small wing from a piece of fly foam and trim to a small V at the rear. Color the bottom side of the foam with permanent markers to match the body color.
Step 4: Tie wing in at the head. Place a drop of Super Glue on the underside of the wing and hold down until it is secured to the body. Finish head and cement to complete the Foam-Wing Caddis.

Gray Wulff

The Wulff series of flies are great general imitators for fast moving water. They imitate mayflies and caddisflies when fished over broken water, and some of the Wullfs are also excellent as attractors. For example; the Royal Wulff.

The Gray Wulff is one of my favorites in the rivers and streams around the Northwest, as it is in most western states.

Hook: Daiichi 1170, sizes 10-16
Thread: Gray 6/0
Tail: Deer or elk hair
Body: Muskrat fur or gray synthetic dubbing
Wing: Deer or elk hair
Hackle: Dark blue dun

Tying Steps
Step 1: Tie in a tail of deer or elk hair.
Step 2: Tie in the wing, upright and divided.
Step 3: Dub on the body to the back of the wings.

Step 4: Tie in a couple dark dun hackles and wind forward.
Step 5: Finish head and cement to complete the Gray Wulff.

Royal Trude

The Royal Trude is one of those "strawberry shortcake" patterns—an attractor that for some reason or another works very well, especially on fast moving rivers and mountain streams.

Hook: Daiich 1170, sizes 8-16
Thread: Black
Tail: Golden pheasant tippets
Rib: Gold wire
Body: Peacock herl/red floss/peacock herl
Wing: White calf tail
Hackle: Coachman brown

Tying Steps
Step 1: Tie in the tail.
Step 2: Wind on peacock herl up the rear 1/3 of the hook shank. Tie in a piece of fine gold wire and floss. Wind the floss forward, then the wire, and complete the body by winding the last 1/3 of the body with

more peacock herl.
Step 3: Secure a wing of white calf tail.
Step 4: Tie in a couple quality neck hackles and wind on nice and thick. Finish head and cement to complete the Royal Trude

Dave's Hopper

During the heat of summer when grasshoppers are out, tossing these terrestrials to the banks of a stream often produces some hot and heavy action.

There are many hopper imitations on the market. The one featured here is a slightly modified Dave's Hopper. It is a pattern that has been in my fly box for years, and is my all-time favorite.

Hook: Daiichi 1280, sized 6-12
Thread: Black 3/0
Tail: Scarlet hackle fibers
Body: Light yellow poly yarn
Rib: Brown hackle, clipped
Legs: Dyed yellow grizzly hackle stems, clipped and knotted
Underwing: Yellow calf tail
Wing: Turkey quill
Collar: Deer hair

Head: Deer hair, spun and clipped.
Tying Steps
Step 1: Tie in the tail of scarlet hackle fibers.
Step 2: Secure a brown hackle by the tip and tie in the poly yarn. Wind poly yarn forward and secure. Wind hackle forward and secure. Clip hackle to length of hook gape.
Step 3: Tie in an underwing of yellow

calf tail. Then in the wing of turkey quill.
Step 4: Tie in your clipped and knotted hackle stems for the legs.
Step 5: Secure the deer hair as a collar.
Step 6: Spin and clip deer hair to form the head, whip finish and cement to complete Dave's Hopper.

Termite

During fall, from the western slopes of the Cascade Mountains to the ocean there are a great number of termites flying around. Whenever they are present, trout in rivers and lakes will key in on these abundant pests.

I came up with this pattern by necessity while camping at a western reservoir. Trout were rising voraciously taking the hapless adults after their flight path went amuck. I whipped up a few of these imitations and bingo...we were into the fish.

Hook: Daiichi 1280, size 10
Thread: Brown
Body: Brown chenille or dubbing
Wing: Elk body hair
Hackle: Brown neck

Tying Steps

Step 1: Tie on a piece of brown chenille and wind on the rear section of the body.

Step 2: Tie in a neck hackle and wind 2 or 3 turns.

Step 3: Secure a wing of light elk body hair.

Step 4: Tie in another piece of brown chenille and wind on the forward body section. Finish head and cement to complete the Termite.

Irish's Baetis

During fall, one of the most prevalent hatches in many Northwest rivers is the *Baetis* mayfly. On the Yakima River, the tiny BWO is your key to success. Tim Irish, the Yakima's first trout guide, designed this *Baetis* pattern for those fall hatches. Tim doesn't guide the Yakima anymore, but his legend, and Baetis pattern live on.

Fish it along the banks and current seams on a long, fine tippet, using a drag-free drift.

Hook: Daiichi 1140, size 20
Thread: 8/0 olive
Tail: Dun neck hackle
Body: Olive dubbing
Wing Post: Orange poly yarn
Hackle: Dun neck hackle, parachute-style

Tying Steps

Step 1: Tie in a wing post of orange poly yarn.

Step 2: Place a small amount of dubbing material on your thread and wrap a couple turns.

Step 3: Tie in a few dun hackle fibers behind the dubbing for the tail.

Step 4: Secure a dun neck hackle to the wing post.

Step 5: Place more dubbing on the thread and wind forward.

Step 6: Wind hackle 2 or 3 turns, whip finish and cement head to complete Irish's Baetis.

Stimulator

The Stimulator is one of the best adult stonefly and traveling sedge (caddis) patterns ever created. It also does a fair job when the fish are on hoppers. It is very suggestive, floats well and works everywhere stonefly hatches occur. By simply changing the size and color of this fly you can imitate any stonefly hatch. Enough said!

Hook: Daiichi 1280, or 1270, sizes 6-12
Thread: Orange
Tail: Moose mane
Abdomen: Yellow (or color to match what you are imitating) synthetic dubbing or yarn
Rib: Brown or grizzly hackle, palmered
Thorax: Yellow or orange synthetic
Wing: Elk or deer body hair

Hackle: Grizzly, palmered through thorax

Tying Steps

Step 1: Tie in a tail of moose mane or elk or deer body hair.

Step 2: Tie in a hackle by the tip and dub your thread or tie in a piece of wool yarn to be used for the abdomen.

Step 3: Wind body forward stopping 3/4 the way up the hook shank. Now wind the hackle forward.

Step 4: Tie in a wing of elk or deer body hair.

Step 5: Tie in more body material and another hackle in front of the wing.

Step 6: Wind thorax forward and secure. Wind hackle over thorax.

Step 7: Finish head and cement to complete the Stimulator.

Salmonfly

When the giant salmonflies hatch around the West, they create a commotion for top-water feeding that is unparalleled by any other insect. At least, the adults are so big, and the takes by feeding trout are so violent—it seems that way.

Anglers come out of the woodwork to fish salmonfly hatches. Some fly fishers I know, only fish the salmonfly hatches, and then hang up their rods—they say nothing can compare. I say they are a bit loony, but there is something about trout splashing all over the surface taking these giant stonefly adults.

Every Western fly tier has their own version of the perfect salmonfly. Here is mine.

Hook: Daiichi 1280, or 1273, size 6 or 8
Thread: Orange
Tail: Brown goose biots
Body: Orange yarn or synthetic dubbing
Hackle: Brown neck
Wing: Commercial plastic wing material

Antennae: Brown goose biots

Tying Steps
Step 1: Tie in 2 goose biots so they oppose, as seen in the finished fly.
Step 2: Tie in a quality brown neck hackle by the tip, and a piece of yarn, or place dubbing on your thread.
Step 3: Wind body forward, and then palmer the hackle up the body and secure.
Step 4: Cut 2 plastic wings and tie in as shown on the finished fly.
Step 5: Tie in 2 goose biots facing towards the rear of the fly and 2 facing forward. Finish head and cement to complete the Salmonfly.

Griffith's Gnat

This fly is one of the best imitations of small, adult insects around. Whether midges, mayflies or caddisflies, when they are small, the Griffith's Gnat is a good choice for imitating them.

The traditional Griffith's Gnat is tied with the hackle untrimmed. I have found by trimming the hackle top and bottom the fly rides low in the surface film and, I personally find it more effective.

Hook: Daiichi 1100, size 16 or 18
Thread: Black or olive 8/0

Body: Peacock herl
Hackle: Grizzly neck hackle

Step 1: Secure 2 or 3 strands of peacock herl and 1 quality neck hackle to the hook as shown.

Step 2: Wind herl forward.

Step 3: Wind hackle forward and whip finish head.

Step 4: Trim hackle top and bottom and cement head to complete the Griffith's Gnat.

Iridescent Black Cricket

Terrestrials seem to work magic wherever they are fished. Trout will often take terrestrials even during the hatch of an aquatic insect. Crickets have long been a favorite terrestrial fly pattern.

The Iridescent Black Cricket, a pattern by Ronn Lucas, Sr., is a realistic tie that simply can't be refused by any self-respecting trout when floated along a grassy bank.

Hook: Daiichi 1270, size 10
Thread: Black 6/0
Tail: Black stripped quills
Antenna: Stripped finely barred grizzly hackle stems
Eyes: Iridescent black beads & mono
Abdomen: Black #202 Foamback wound around the hook, or, dyed black deer or elk hair
Rear Legs: Black dyed, knotted pheasant tail
Wing, Thorax and Head: Dyed black turkey.
Thorax and Front Legs: #2 black Iridescent Dubbing, picked out with teaser or bodkin

Tying Steps
Note: The following sequence of steps are my version, not necessarily the order in which the designer, Ronn Lucas, might put this fly together.
Step 1: Tie in the black stripped quills for the tail.
Step 2: Tie in foam and wind forward 1/2 way up the hook and secure.
Step 3: Tie in the pheasant tail legs.
Step 4: Secure a section of dyed black turkey quill so it extends down the abdomen as shown. Leave the rest of the quill section intact for later use.
Step 5: Tie in the antenna of hackle stems.

Step 6: Dub on the thorax. After the thorax is built up slightly, tie in the eyes. Continue building up the thorax with dubbing material ending up with your tying thread behind the eyes.
Step 7: Pull turkey quill forward and secure behind the eyes. Work the tying thread through the dubbing to the head.
Step 8: Tie down the remaining turkey quill, trim off excess, pick out dubbing on the underside of the fly with a dubbing teaser or bodkin, whip finish and cement, to complete the Iridescent Black Cricket.

Foam Ant

This is a high-floating ant pattern that, like most ants, trout find irresistible. When high visibility is what you are after, it's hard to beat this little terrestrial.

Hook: Daiichi 1110, size 16
Thread: Black
Body: Precut ant foam
Hackle: Black neck

Tying Steps
Step 1: Secure thread to the center of the hook and wind on a base.
Step 2: Tie in a foam body, securing so the rear section is slightly larger than the front.
Step 3: Tie in a quality neck hackle and wind 2 turns. Whip finish and cement to complete the Foam Ant.

Thread Ant

Unlike the Foam Ant, Thread Ants sink down a bit and resemble drowned ants. There are times when these "drowned ants" work better than the high floaters.

Hook: Daiichi 1180, size 16
Thread: Black 8/0
Body: Tying thread
Hackle: Black neck

Step 1: Wind on the rear segment with the tying thread as shown.

Step 2: Tie in a quality neck hackle.

Step 3: Wind hackle 2 turns.

Step 4: Wind on the forward segment and whip finish.

Step 5: Coat entire body with a couple coats of head cement to complete the Thread Ant.

Deer Hair Beetle

Another terrestrial that every small stream fly fisher should have in their box. Like the ant, this fly often works even during the midst of a hatch.

Hook: Daiichi 1180 or 1190, sizes 10-14
Thread: Black
Body: Black deer body hair
Legs/Antenna: Black deer body hair
Hi-Vis indicator: Tuft of orange poly yarn

Tying Steps
Step 1: Secure a small bunch of deer hair to the hook wrapping it down to the bend of the hook.
Step 2: Pull hair forward forming a shell-like appearance and secure 3/4 the way up the hook shank. Pull back 4 hairs and pin with tying thread forming the back legs. Trim off the excess.
Step 3: Tie in another small bunch of deer hair, this time winding the thread forward, securing the hairs to the head.

Step 4: Leave 2 hairs facing forward for the antenna, and pull the remaining hair back towards the other body segment, and secure, forming the head. Pin 4 hairs with your tying thread forming more legs. Trim off excess.
Step 5: Tie in a small tuft of orange poly yarn where the two segments meet, whip finish and cement to complete the Deer Hair Beetle.

Foam-Head Stillborn Chironomid

Midges are the most abundant and important food item in lakes during spring. The Chironomid midge is the most important to the fly fisher. It is the pupal stage of this insect that is the most vulnerable to the trout, and consequently the most important to imitate for lake fishing.

When the Chironomid pupa rises to the surface, it splits along the back and the adult hatches out. Sometimes the hatch doesn't complete, leaving the stillborn in the surface film. This fly imitates this occurrence.

One of the biggest obstacles in Chironomid fishing is seeing the tiny insect on the water. Some anglers use strike indicators, some grease their leader with fly floatant. I started tying my stillborn pupas with a foam head so I can actually keep an eye on the fly. When it disappears there is no mistake that a fish has sipped it in.

Hook: Daiichi 1273, sizes 10-18
Thread: Black, brown or olive 6/0
Tail: Fluff from the base of a grizzly hackle
Abdomen: V-RIB (match color of natural Chironomids)
Thorax: Peacock herl
Hackle: Grizzly
Foam Head: Fly Foam

Step 1: Tie in a small tuft of grizzly hackle "fluff" from the base of a grizzly hackle.

Step 2: Secure a piece of V-RIB as shown with the rounded side down.

Step 3: Wind V-RIB forward to form the abdomen and secure.

Step 4: Cut a small piece of fly foam and secure at the head of the fly.

Step 5: Place a drop of Super Glue on the foam to secure.

Step 6: Tie in 3 or 4 strands of peacock herl in front of the abdomen.

Step 7: Wind the herl forward to form the thorax.

Step 8: Tie in a neck hackle behind the foam head.

Step 9: Wind the hackle 1 turn, finish head and cement to complete the Foam Head Stillborn Chironomid.

Super Floss Chironomid Pupa

Being one of the most important patterns to the lake fly fisher it is not surprising that there are so many Chironomid pupa imitations out there. For the most part, it is a simple pattern to tie and, a variety of materials can be used in the tying process.

I have experimented, like most tiers, with a plethora of styles and materials. Most of my standard pupa imitations these days are tied with an abdomen of Super Floss, a material that is about as easy to work with as any I have used. With its ability to stretch it is great for tying extremely small patterns.

Chironomid pupas can be fished from top to bottom. Most anglers fish them on, or near the surface by greasing their leader with fly floatant. When trout are taking the naturals on the surface, the rings will appear as if it were raining. But don't be afraid during those slow periods to sink a Chironomid pupa to the bottom and dance it just above the muck. Sometimes this is the key to success.

Hook: Daiichi 1560, sizes 12-18
Thread: Dark olive (match body color)
Abdomen: Dark olive (match naturals on water)
Rib: Pearl Flashabou or Krystal Flash
Thorax: Flash dubbing or any synthetic dubbing with sparkle
Wing case: Turkey quill
Gills: Poly yarn

Step 1: Secure a piece of Super Floss and a strand of pearl Flashabou or Krystal Flash as shown.

Step 2: Wind Super Floss Forward forming the abdomen.

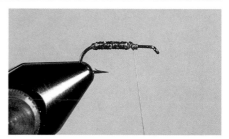

Step 3: Wind ribbing forward.

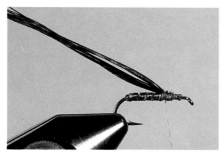

Step 4: Tie in a section of turkey quill in front of the abdomen.

Step 5: Dub on the thorax with your favorite dubbing.

Step 6: Secure a small tuft of poly yarn in front of the thorax using a figure eight motion of the tying thread.

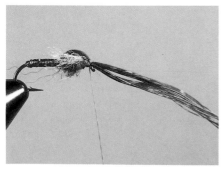

Step 7: Pull quill forward and secure, forming the wing case.

Step 8: Clip off excess quill, trim the poly yarn so that it extends to 1/16" on each side, finish head and cement to complete the Super Floss Chironomid Pupa.

Larva Lace Chironomid Pupa

Another popular body material, Larva Lace stretches easily for tying pupas on a variety of hook sizes. This material comes in a variety of colors.

Red Chironomid Pupa

Earth tones; black, brown, olive, etc. are the most popular colors for tying Chironomids. Low oxygen waters will host larva and pupa in shades of red. Anglers wise to this are wise indeed.

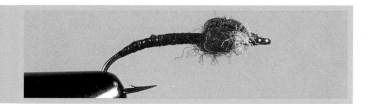

Micro Midge Pupa

There are times when extremely small midges are hatching and the trout will have nothing to do with anything but the tiny insects. This often happens during the heat of summer, and many anglers fail to catch fish because they have no midge pupas small enough, or, fail to recognize that this is what the fish are feeding on.

Obviously, light tippets and a delicate touch are called for when fishing tiny midges, but they just might save your bacon when fishing over stubborn trout

Hook: Daiichi J220, sizes 20-24
Body: Black tying thread
Head: Black ostrich herl

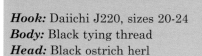

Step 1: Form a small body of tying thread and cement.

Step 2: Tie in 1 strand of ostrich herl at head.

Step 3: Wind herl 1 or 2 turns and secure. Whip finish head to complete the Micro Midge Pupa.

Brassie

The Brassie is a great pattern when trout are feeding on midge larvae and pupae in moving water. This fly works especially well when dead-drifted along the bottom for picky fish, like those found in spring creeks and heavily fished waters.

Hook: Daiichi 1270, sizes 16-22
Thread: Black, 6/0
Abdomen: Copper wire
Head: Peacock herl

Tying Steps
Step 1: Secure the tying thread and wrap the hook shank from butt to head.
Step 2: Secure a piece of fine copper wire along the hook shank and wrap with thread, creating an even base for the abdomen.
Step 3: Wind the wire forward in tight wraps and secure three-quarters up the hook shank.
Step 4: Tie in a strand of peacock herl and wind on the thorax. Finish head and cement to complete the Brassie.

Super Floss Ascending Midge Pupa

When midge larvae pupate and rise to the surface they are very vulnerable to the feeding trout. While most anglers seem to fish midges only on, or near the surface, they are sometimes missing out on a feeding frenzy taking place below.

In still waters, the Ascending Midge Pupa should be fished from the bottom to then top, using whatever line it takes to accomplish this. What I like to do is cast an ascending pupa out on a full-sinking line, and slowly draw it to the surface, pausing often with the retrieve.

Hook: Daiichi 1550, sizes 12-18

Thread: Black 8/0
Abdomen: Super Floss (browns, black, olives)
Thorax: Sparkle dubbing (your favorite dubbing, to match or slightly darker than abdomen)
Hackle: Hen neck (any small soft hackle feather)

Step 1: Wind on an abdomen of Super Floss as shown.

Step 2: Dub on a thorax of your favorite dubbing.

Step 3: Secure a small soft hackle feather in front of the thorax.

Step 4: Wind hackle 2 or 3 turns, finish head and cement to complete the Super Floss Ascending Midge Pupa.

San Juan Worm

There are those fly fishers who turn their nose up at the thought of using a San Juan Worm. "An imitation of a worm...really!" Although those same fly fishers have no problem using imitations of other food items of the trout; mayflies, scuds, grasshoppers, ants, etc. I don't get it.

The San Juan Worm imitates the larval stage of the midge. It is best fished when danced right along the bottom of a lake, or dead drifted along the bottom of a slow section of a stream.

Although not as popular in many northwestern waters as it is in the Rocky Mountain states, the SJW works very well for our Northwest trout.

Red San Juan Worm

Hook: Daiichi 1150, sizes 8-16
Thread: Match body color
Body: Vernille, red, brown or orange

Step 1: Secure a base of thread on your hook and secure a short piece of Vernille at the butt of the hook as shown.

Step 2: Wind your thread forward and secure the Vernille at the head of the fly as shown.

Step 3: With a match or other heat source, melt the ends of the Vernille into a tapered "worm" shape. Whip finish thread and cement to complete the San Juan Worm.

Bead Head Soft Hackle

Soft-hackle flies have become quite popular over the years. They are great imitators of ascending pupas as well as a variety of other aquatic food items. Bead head flies have become quite popular also.

With this fly I combined the effectiveness of a soft hackle with that of a gold bead head, and threw in some time-proven peacock herl for good measure. The result is one of my favorite soft hackle flies for lake fishing.

Fish this fly around weed beds with a slow retrieve. During those hatchless periods when you are looking for something to try, give the Bead Head Soft Hackle a shot. It has saved the day for me...more than once!

Hook: Daiichi 1273, sizes 8-16
Thread: Dark Olive
Tail: Dark hen hackle or partridge
Body: Peacock herl
Ribbing: Gold Mylar or tinsel
Hackle: Dark hen hackle or partridge

Bead Head: 1/8" gold bead (match bead size to hook size)

Tying Steps
Step 1: Slide a bead onto the hook shank.
Step 2: Tie in a tail of hen hackle or partridge.

Step 3: Wind on a body of peacock herl and rib with Mylar.
Step 4: Secure a hen hackle just behind the bead and wind two or three turns.
Step 5: Whip finish behind the bead and cement to complete the Bead Head Soft Hackle.

Bug-Eye Nymph

Sometimes at the bench, experimenting, you come up with a fly that just looks "fishy." This pattern is the result of just such a thing.

The Bug-Eye Nymph doesn't really resemble anything, but it looks alive and "buggy" in the water, at least, enough to fool trout in both rivers and still waters.

I have used this fly from the Rockies to the remotes of the Yukon—it is a pattern that I am never without. It can be fished from top to bottom with equal results.

Hook: Daiichi 2421 size 10 or 12
Thread: Black
Tail: Grizzly hackle fibers
Abdomen: Black dubbing (your favorite)
Ribbing: Silver wire
Thorax: Black dubbing
Hackle: Grizzly
Eyes: Silver bead chain

Tying Steps
Step 1: Tie in grizzly hackle fibers for the tail.
Step 2: Tie in a piece of silver wire to be used as a rib.
Step 3: Dub on the abdomen, stopping 3/4 the way up the hook shank.
Step 4: Wind rib forward.
Step 5: Tie in 1 grizzly neck hackle by the tip in front of the abdomen.

Step 6: Secure small bead-chain eyes at the head using a figure-eight motion of the tying thread.
Step 7: Dub on a thorax, slightly thicker than the abdomen.
Step 8: Wind hackle forward and secure behind the bead-chain eyes.
Step 9: Whip finish behind the eyes, and cement to complete the Bug-Eye Nymph.

Bead Head Caddis Larva

Caddisflies are found everywhere and, caddisfly larvae are a staple in the diet of trout found in many rivers. These abundant little morsels tumble along the stream bottom when dislodged from the rocks. Trout seldom refuse a properly fished caddis imitation.

The short-line nymphing technique is a good way to fish this fly. With a strike indicator up your leader about twice the distance as the water is deep, follow the fly's drift with your rod tip. When you feel any abnormal movement in the indicator, set the hook.

Hook: Daiichi 1710 sizes 6-14
Thread: Black or gray
Body: Dubbed muskrat fur with hairs left in.
Bead Head: Gold bead.

Tying Steps
Step 1: Secure thread to the hook and slide a gold bead up the hook shank.
Step 2: Dub on a thick body of muskrat fur with hairs included.

Step 3: Whip finish behind the bead and cement to complete the Bead Head Caddis Larva.

Waterboatman

The water boatman is important at times to the stillwater fly fisher. The boatman gets it name from its oar-like legs that appear to be rowing as it moves through the water.

Trout don't always key in on the naturals, but when they do, those without a few boatman imitations are out of luck. Imitations should be fished near the surface with erratic movements to mimic the naturals.

Hook: Daiichi 1270, sizes 12-18
Thread: Brown 6/0
Body: Light brown Flash Dubbing, or any sparkle dubbing
Shellback: Turkey quill
Legs: Single feather fiber from turkey quill

Tying Steps
Step 1: Tie in a section of turkey quill to be used for the shellback.
Step 2: Wind on dubbing to form the body. 3/4 the way up the hook shank, tie in 1 quill fiber on each side for the legs, and finish dubbing on the body.

Step 3: Pull turkey quill section forward and secure, finish head.
Step 4: Lacquer the top of the shellback several times until it retains a high gloss, to complete the Waterboatman.

Carey Special

My first fly-caught trout was taken on a Carey Special. Needless to say, this is a special fly pattern for me. This fly has long been a standard lake pattern, generally imitating important food items such as damselfly and dragonfly nymphs and caddis pupa.

This is a fly that can be tied using a plethora of materials. Virtually any body material or color can be used. You can add a tail, ribbing, bead head, etc. My favorite is a simple, plain-looking Carey. It remains to this day, one of my favorite search patterns when fishing lakes.

Hook: Daiichi 2421, sizes 6-12.
Thread: Black
Body: Crystal Chenille, Cactus Chenille, or your favorite
Hackle: Ring-necked pheasant rump feather

Tying Steps
Step 1: Tie in your body material and wind forward.
Step 2: Secure a pheasant rump feather and wind several turns.

Step 3: Finish head and cement to complete the Carey Special.

Caddis Pupa

The caddis is one of the most important food items for trout. Most fly fishers are very familiar with adult caddis patterns, but many fail to recognize the importance of the underwater stages—the larva and pupa. It is the pupal stage of the caddis that is probably the most overlooked.

When the caddis pupates and ascends to the surface it becomes very vulnerable. Imitations should be fished with a slow retrieve in still waters. In rivers, the down-and-across approach is effective as it allows the fly to rise on the swing, which does a good job of imitating the ascending pupa.

Hook: Daiichi 1270, sizes 6-20
Thread: Black
Body: Sparkle Dubbing, Antron, or your favorite, in tan, brown, olive, etc. (colors vary on the naturals, it's good to carry a selection)

Hackle: Hen neck or partridge
Head: Black dubbing

Tying Steps
Step 1: Dub on a body 3/4 the way up the hook shank.

Step 2: Tie in a hen hackle and wind 2 turns.
Step 3: Dub on the head, whip finish and cement to complete the Caddis Pupa.

Prince Nymph

The Prince Nymph has long been a popular stream pattern in the western states. Although not so popular in the Northwestern U.S., it is nonetheless a very good search pattern in rivers and streams all around the west.

Like Hare's Ear and Pheasant Tail Nymphs, the Prince should be in every fly fisher's nymph box. Although it doesn't closely imitate any natural foods, it generally emulates several food items, like mayfly and stonefly nymphs.

Hook: Daiichi 1710, sizes 10-8
Thread: Tail: Brown goose biots
Rib: Fine flat gold tinsel
Body: Peacock herl
Hackle: Brown hackle
Wings: White goose biots

Tying Steps
Step 1: Tie in 2 goose biots for the tail.
Step 2: Wind on a body of peacock herl and rib with gold tinsel.
Step 3: Tie in a brown hackle and

wind a few turns, securing most of the fibers underneath the hook "beard style".
Step 4: Tie in 2 white biots flat on top of the body, finish head and cement to complete the Prince Nymph.

Iridescent Flashback Stonefly Nymph

Stonefly nymphs are abundant in moving waters around the Northwest and are a favorite food item of the trout. These nymphs are available the year around, so trout are plenty familiar with them.

The Iridescent Flashback Stonefly Nymph is another Ronn Lucas Sr., pattern that is very suggestive of the real thing, and has proven very effective on trout. Stonefly nymphs are best fished using a short-line nymphing technique, dead drifted along the bottom of a rocky stream.

Hook: Daiichi 2340, sizes 2-8.
Thread: Brown (black for black nymphs)
Tail: Brown goose biots
Abdomen: Brown Iridescent Dubbing (black for black nymphs)
Ribbing: Brown Swannundaze (black for black nymphs)
Wingcase: Flashback
Antenna: Stripped hackle stems
Eyes: Iridescent black beads & mono.
Legs: Brown saddle hackle (black for black nymphs)

Thorax: Brown Iridescent Dubbing

Tying Steps
Note: These tying steps are my sequence, not those of the designer, Ronn Lucas, Sr.
Step 1: Tie in goose biots for the tail.
Step 2: Secure a piece of Swannundaze to the hook, dub on the abdomen and wind the Swannundaze forward as a rib.
Step 3: Tie in the antenna and eyes.
Step 4: Secure a piece of Flashback

and cut to shape as seen in the finished fly. Tie in a brown saddle hackle by the tip.
Step 5: Dub on the thorax and weave the hackle forward through the dubbing, securing behind the eyes.
Step 6: Weaving your tying thread back through the dubbed thorax secure more Flashback as seen in the finished fly. Cut to shape and secure behind the eyes, whip finish and cement to complete the Iridescent Flashback Stonefly Nymph.

Snail

Most stillwater anglers don't think about snails as being forage for trout. I didn't really think about it much myself until Gary Borger enlightened me one time at an FFF Conclave. Today I am never without a selection of snails whenever fishing lakes around the Northwest.

This snail pattern is one designed by Gary Borger. The colors and shape do a good job of imitating the naturals, the hackle is there to grab the fish's attention. It should be lightly twitched around shallow weedbeds or anywhere snails are found.

Hook: Daiichi 1150, sizes 12-16
Thread: Black
Underbody: lead wire
Overbody: Peacock herl
Ribbing: Copper wire
Hackle: Brown neck

Tying Steps
Step 1: Wind on an underbody of lead wire, then attach 3 strands of peacock herl and a short piece of copper wire.
Step 2: Wind herl forward forming a

rounded snail shape. Wind wire forward and secure.
Step 3: Tie in 1 quality neck hackle and wind 1 turn. Finish head and cement to complete the Snail.

Gold Ribbed Hare's Ear Nymph

This fly is one you can find in nearly every fly tying book out there but I feel it is such an important pattern in Northwest waters I couldn't "not include" it in this book.

When tied in various sizes and colors the Gold Ribbed Hare's Ear Nymph resembles a variety of aquatic foods including mayfly and stonefly nymphs, damselfly nymphs, scuds, caddis, etc. The standard Hare's Ear is one of the best all-round *Callibaetis* mayfly nymph general imitations there is. And since the *Callibaetis* mayfly is present in most of our Northwest waters, it's simply a good choice.

The Hare's Ear is also one of my favorite "search" patterns, one I use most often when fishing unknown waters or during times of no hatch. It can be fished from top to bottom in rivers and in still waters.

Many tiers tie this nymph using bead heads or flashback style. It lends itself well to many variations.

Hook: Daiichi 1710, sizes 8-18
Thread: Brown or tan 6/0
Tail: Hare's mask guard hair fibers or hen hackle fibers
Abdomen: Hare's mask dubbing (without guard hairs)
Ribbing: Gold, oval or flat tinsel or wire
Thorax: Hare's mask dubbing (including guard hairs)
Wing case: Turkey wing

Step 1: Tie in a short tail of guard hairs from the forehead of an English hare's mask.

Step 2: Tie in the oval, gold tinsel as shown.

Step 3: Dub on a tight abdomen of hare's mask fur 3/4 the way up the hook shank.

Step 4: Wind tinsel forward and secure.

Step 5: Secure a section of turkey quill as shown.

Step 6: Dub on a thorax of hare's mask fur with guard hairs included, to resemble the legs of the nymph.

Step 7: Pull turkey quill forward and secure to form the wing case.

Step 8: Finish head and cement to complete the Gold Ribbed Hare's Ear Nymph.

Plastic-Back Scud

Whenever scuds are present in a lake, or spring creek, they will be among the favorite food items of the trout. These numerous little crustaceans wiggle erratically, seemingly struggling to move. A properly fished imitation will do the same.

Scuds live around shallow shoreline vegetation and structure. Obviously, that's where you should fish them. The pick-up is often subtle, so you need to stay on your toes.

Hook: Daiichi 1155, sizes 12-16
Thread: Olive
Body: Olive dubbing (try different shades of olive)
Rib: Copper wire
Shellback: Plastic bag strip

Tying Steps
Step 1: Tie in a piece of copper wire and a plastic strip approximately 1/8" wide (depending on fly size)
Step 2: Dub on a loose body of Antron (or your favorite) dubbing.

Step 3: Pull shellback forward and secure.
Step 4: Wind ribbing forward and secure, finish head.
Step 5: With a dubbing teaser or bodkin, pick out the dubbing giving a ragged effect to the bottom of the fly.

Iridescent Flashback Scud

The Iridescent Flashback Scud, tied by Ronn Lucas, Sr., is the best scud imitation I have ever used—hands down! Tied with relatively new materials, this scud will produce anywhere scuds and trout are found.

Experiment with different colors. Must scuds will found in shades of olive. Also experiment with hook sizes. Trout can be extremely fussy when it comes to this.

Hook: Daiichi 1150, sizes 12-16
Thread: 6/0 olive (match body color)
Tail: Olive hackle fibers
Body: Iridescent dubbing, #30 med. olive (or color to suit)
Rib: Wire, color to suit
Eyes: Green beads and mono
Antennae: Olive hackle fibers

Tying Steps
Step 1: Tie in a short tail of hackle fibers.
Step 2: Secure antennae at eye of hook and tie in bead eyes.
Step 3: Tie in a piece of Flashback #110 (or color to suit) and place dubbing on your thread.

Step 4: Wind dubbing forward, then pull shellback forward and secure.
Step 5: Wind wire forward, secure, finish head and cement.
Step 6: With a dubbing teaser or bodkin, pick out dubbing on the bottom of the fly to look as shown, to complete the Iridescent Flashback Scud.

Tellico Nymph

The Tellico is a pattern that you don't see too often in fly boxes around the Northwest. Admittedly, this isn't my first-out pattern under most situations either, but there are a few situations where I would feel lost without a few Tellicos in my fly box.

During late fall when wasps are annoyingly aggressive, and dying, they often find their way into streams and eventually into the mouths of trout. I have spent many fall afternoons casting Tellico Nymphs that, I'm sure, were being taken for drowned wasps.

Another occasion for a Tellico Nymph to find its way to my tippet is when fishing the alpine lakes. I'm not sure what the trout are taking this nymph for there, but it certainly seems to excite those mountain trout.

Hook: Daiichi 1530, sizes 6-16
Thread: Black
Tail: Guinea feather fibers
Body: Yellow dubbing
Rib: Peacock herl
Shellback: Ring-necked pheasant tail fibers
Hackle: Brown hen

Tying Steps
Step 1: Tie in a short tail of guinea feather fibers.
Step 2: Secure the pheasant fibers for the shellback and peacock herl for the rib at the butt of the fly.
Step 3: Dub on the body, wind the

ribbing forward, and pull the shellback forward, securing at the head of the fly.
Step 4: Tie in a hen neck feather and wind 1 turn.
Step 5: Finish head and cement to complete the Tellico Nymph.

Flash-Back Pheasant Tail Nymph

The Pheasant Tail Nymph is one of those flies that just seems to work everywhere for trout. It is one of the most reliable nymphs ever designed, generally imitating mayfly nymphs, small stonefly nymphs, scuds, etc.

Very popular variations from the standard Pheasant Tail Nymph are the Bead-Head Pheasant Tail and the Flash-Back Pheasant Tail. In my opinion you should have all three in your nymph box, and in assorted sizes, at all times.

Hook: Daiichi 1710, sizes 6-16
Thread: Copper, brown or black
Tail: Pheasant tail fibers
Abdomen: Pheasant tail fibers
Ribbing: Fine copper wire
Thorax: Peacock herl
Legs: Pheasant tail fibers
Wingcase: Pearl Sea Flash, or iridescent pearl tape

Top View

Step 1: Tie in pheasant tail fibers for a tail.

Step 2: Tie in a longer bunch of pheasant tail fibers to be used for the abdomen, and a fine copper wire to be used for the rib.

Step 3: Wind on the abdomen.

Step 4: Wind ribbing in the opposite direction you wound on the pheasant tail.

Step 5: Secure a piece of iridescent tape or similar product for the wingcase.

Step 6: Tie in a few strands of peacock herl to be used for the wingcase.

Step 7: Wind herl forward forming the thorax.

Step 8: Tie in 3 pheasant tail fibers on each side of the hook as shown, forming the legs of the nymph.

Step 9: Pull the wingcase material forward and secure, finish head and cement to complete the Flash-Back Pheasant Tail Nymph.

Zug Bug

Like the Gold Ribbed Hare's Ear Nymph, the Zug Bug is a pattern that I just couldn't leave out of this book, even though it is included in many other books. This is one that you simply should not be without.

Fished in the same manner as the Hare's Ear Nymph, the Zug Bug generally imitates food items like mayfly and damselfly nymphs, caddis pupae, etc. One thing that contributes to the effectiveness of this fly, I'm sure, is all the peacock herl used in the tying process.

Hook: Daiichi 1710, sizes 6-16
Thread: Black or olive
Tail: Peacock herl
Body: Peacock herl
Rib: Oval silver tinsel
Hackle: Furnace, sparse, tied beard-style
Wingcase: Woodduck flank or turkey quill, clipped short

Step 1: Tie in a short tail of peacock herl.

Step 2: Secure a piece of oval silver tinsel and several strands of peacock herl as shown.

Step 3: Wind herl forward to form the body.

Step 4: Wind tinsel forward.

Step 5: Tie a furnace hackle in at the head.

Step 6: Wind the hackle a couple turns pulling the fibers to the bottom of the hook and securing as a beard. Tie in a section of woodduck flank or turkey quill as shown.

Step 7: Clip quill short forming a wingcase, finish head and cement to complete the Zug Bug.

Woolly Bugger

It has been said countless times by countless anglers..."if I only had one fly to fish with, anywhere, anytime, it would be the Woolly Bugger." I tend to agree. This fly simply catches a lot of fish.

The Woolly Bugger can be fished from top to bottom using a variety of techniques. More often than not it is fished with a sinking line and is probably taken as a leech by the trout. A slow retrieve is the key.

Although black, brown and olive are the most widely tied colors of Buggers, you can tie this fly in virtually any color, any size, and using a variety of materials, making this fly effective for a variety of fish.

For example; a Woolly Bugger tied in yellow, on a size 12 hook is great for panfish. An olive Bugger on a standard streamer hook is one of the best patterns there is for trout in lakes, and a big purple Bugger size 2/0 is one of my favorite steelhead flies. This is simply one of the most versatile patterns that has ever been created.

It can be tied using the standard body of chenille, dubbing, leech yarn—the sky's the limit. Adding a few strands of Krystal Flash or Holographic Flash along the body and extending to the length of the tail gives this fly a bit of sparkle and a little extra punch when fishing moving water.

Hook: Daiichi 2220 sizes 1-14
Thread: Black
Tail: Black marabou
Body: Black chenille
Hackle: Black saddle

Step 1: Secure a piece of marabou for the tail making sure it extends past the bend of the hook a full body length.

Step 2: Tie in a piece of black chenille and a saddle hackle by the tip as shown.

Step 3: Wind chenille forward forming the body.

Step 4: Wind hackle forward.

Step 5: Finish head and cement to complete the Woolly Bugger.

Egg Sucking Bugger

This fly is one of the best trout patterns you can use when fishing in water where there are spawning salmon present. Leeches will cling on to deposited eggs. The Egg Sucking Bugger does a great job of imitating this.

Also try tying this fly in size 14 with a small egg head when spawning trout are present. Black and purple are the most popular colors.

Hook: Daiichi 2220 sizes 1-14
Thread: Black
Tail: Black marabou with 2 strands of Holographic Flash
Body: Black chenille
Hackle: Black saddle

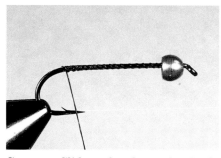

Tying Steps
Tie a basic Woolly Bugger, leaving enough room at the head to form an egg shape out of chenille.

Chickabou Bead Head Bugger

Here is a Woolly Bugger version that has proven very effective—at times, even more so than the conventional tie, which is saying a lot. It combines two of my favorite materials; beads and Chickabou. How could it go wrong?

Hook: Daiichi 2220, sizes 4-10
Thread: Black
Tail: Chickabou
Body: Cactus Chenille
Hackle: Chickabou soft hackle
Bead: 1/8" gold (match fly size with bead)

Step 1: Slide a bead up the hook shank as shown.

Step 2: Tie in 2 or 3 Chickabou feathers for the tail as shown.

Step 3: Tie in a piece of Cactus Chenille and a Chickabou soft hackle by the tip, at the butt of the fly.

Step 4: Wind chenille forward.

Step 5: Wind hackle forward

Step 6: Whip finish behind the bead to complete the Chickabou Bead Head Bugger.

Bead-Head Rubberlegs

Yet another version of the popular Woolly Bugger, this fly has a little more movement, and with the bead head, a little more flash. It's a great river streamer!

Hook: Daiichi 2421, sizes 4-12
Thread: Black
Tail: Black marabou, rubber leg material
Body: Black chenille
Hackle: Black saddle
Legs: Rubber leg material
Bead: Gold (appropriate size for specific hook)

Tying Steps
Step 1: Slide a bead up the hook shank.
Step 2: Tie in a tail of marabou and a couple chunks of rubber leg material.
Step 3: Secure a saddle hackle by the tip and the chenille.

Step 4: Wind chenille forward and palmer hackle to the head.
Step 5: Tie in a couple more chunks of rubber leg material behind the bead head. Whip finish behind the bead and cement to complete the Bead Head Rubberlegs.

Bead Head Woolly Worm

After the Woolly Bugger came along and gained widespread popularity, the Woolly Worm (once just as popular) took a backseat. Fewer and fewer anglers included the Woolly Worm in their boxes.

I seldom carry large Woolly Worms myself, but I do keep a selection in small sizes and, more recently, I have been using bead head-style Woolly Worms.

Fished in both moving and still waters, I find the Bead Head Woolly Worm to be just as effective as the Woolly Bugger at times, especially when fishing them in small sizes. Several colors work well, olive is my favorite for lakes, black for streams.

Hook: Daiichi 1273, sizes 12-18
Thread: Dark olive
Body: Dark olive
Hackle: Grizzly
Bead Head: Silver bead (appropriate size for hook)

Tying Steps
Step 1: Slide the bead up the hook shank to the head.
Step 2: Tie in a piece of chenille along the hook shank, and 1 grizzly hackle by the tip.

Step 3: Wind chenille forward to form the body, and wind the hackle forward, securing at the head.
Step 4: Whip finish behind the bead and cement to complete the Bead Head Woolly Worm.

Damselfly Nymph

Damselfly nymphs are a staple in the diet of still water trout. They can be found in nearly all lakes and ponds. When damsels migrate towards shore in the spring they send trout into a feeding frenzy for sure and, the angler without damsel imitations missed the boat, so to speak.

Fished on a floating, sinking-tip or intermediate line, imitations should be slowly, but erratically retrieved to mimic the undulating movement of the naturals.

I feel the two main features of a good damselfly imitation are movement and eyes. This pattern has plenty of both.

Hook: Daiichi 1273, size 12 or 14
Thread: Olive
Tail: Olive marabou
Abdomen: Olive dubbing

Ribbing: Copper wire
Thorax: Olive dubbing
Hackle: Olive neck
Eyes: Mono Eyes (or melt your own from 50-pound-test monofilament)

Step 1: Tie in a tail of marabou as shown.

Step 2: Tie in a piece of fine copper wire at the butt, and dub your favorite olive dubbing to the tying thread.

Step 3: Wind dubbing forward, stopping 3/4 up the hook shank.

Step 4: Wind copper wire forward.

Step 5: Secure Mono Eyes with a figure-eight motion of the tying thread as shown.

Step 6: Tie in an olive neck hackle by the tip.

Step 7: Dub on a thorax to the eye of the hook.

Step 8: Wind hackle forward and secure *behind* the eyes.

Step 9: Whip finish behind the eyes and cement to complete the Damselfly Nymph.

Dragonfly Nymph

A dragonfly nymph is meat and potatoes to a trout, and many other freshwater species for that matter. This is a big hunk of food present the year around and fish often take advantage of this nutrition.

I feel one of the key elements when tying dragonfly nymphs is making sure you include eyes on the imitation, as they are prominent on the naturals. I tie my imitations with large, commercially-made mono eyes which I feel make this fly so effective.

Dragonfly nymphs should be crawled through weedbeds very slowly to mimic the movement of the naturals. One thing that isn't slow is the take. Be prepared, as trout hit this critter with a vengeance.

Hook: 1720, sizes 4-10
Thread: Olive
Body: Large, olive chenille
Hackle: Dark hen or partridge
Eyes: Large Mono Eyes

Top View

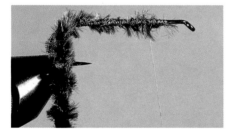

Step 1: Secure a piece of olive chenille along the hook shank as shown.

Step 2: Wind the chenille 3/4 the way up the hook shank and tie off.

Step 4: Tie in another piece of olive chenille behind the eyes and secure.

Step 5: Wind the chenille forward and then back, securing behind the eyes as shown. Clip off excess.

Step 3: Tie in Mono Eyes using a figure-eight motion of the tying thread.

Step 6: Tie in a dyed green soft hackle *behind* the eyes.

Step 7: Wind the hackle 2 or 3 turns, whip finish and cement behind the eyes to complete the Dragonfly Nymph.

Chickabou Leech

When Hoffman Hackles began marketing Chickabou patches, this soft versatile feather started showing up in all sorts of fly patterns. With more action than marabou, it's easy to see why.

I first started using Chickabou feathers as replacement for marabou in a variety of patterns. It found it's way into the tails of my leech patterns, and I eventually started constructing entire leeches of Chickabou feathers. Today, there are several feather growers producing such soft hackles.

Hook: Daiichi 2220 sizes 1-10
Thread: Black
Tail: Brown, black or olive
    Chickabou
Body: Brown, black or olive

Tying Steps
Step 1: Tie in a few Chickabou feathers for the tail.
Step 2: Secure a couple Chickabou feathers and wind forward tightly.

Step 3: Continue winding Chickabou feathers forward until the entire hook shank is covered.
Step 4: Finish head and cement to complete the Chickabou Leech.

Dazzel Leech

Leeches are found nearly everywhere, and they are a prime target for feeding fish. There are a multitude of leech patterns available, one of my favorites is the Dazzel Leech, by Shim Hogan. Like most leeches this is a simple fly to tie. It consists entirely of Dazzel Yarn.

This pattern, like other leeches, should be fished slowly along the bottom and around weedbeds, using whatever line it takes to do so.

Hook: Daiichi 2220, sizes 4-10

Thread: Black
Tail: Dazzel Yarn
Body: Dazzel Yarn

Step 1: Tie in a tail of Dazzel Leech Yarn.

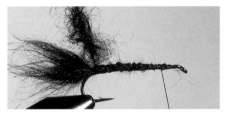

Step 2: Place Dazzel Yarn in your dubbing loop or twist to your thread.

Step 3: Dub on the body (loosely) entirely of Dazzel Yarn.

Step 4: Tie in a wing of Dazzel Yarn.

Step 5: Meld the wing, body and tail together with your fingers and finish head to complete the Dazzel Leech.

Shim's Bead Head Dazzel Leech

Tied in the same manner as the Dazzel Leech, only with a bead head. This fly sinks a little faster, and has a bit of a jigging motion when retrieved.

Night Leech

When the body material Estaz hit the market I started tying leech patterns using this innovative material for the body of my favorite leech pattern. The results were most favorable. Fishing during darkness, a few of my buddies finned side-by-side in float tubes. We were all using leech patterns, but those of us who were using the leeches tied with the Estaz for the body out-fished the leeches tied with more conventional body materials. Coincidence? I don't think so. Numerous outings under the same circumstances proved to us that, at least at night, leeches tied with Estaz for the body outproduced all others...hands down!

Over the years I have used Night Leeches not only for night fishing, but anytime I am fishing in waters that I know contain big trout, such as the pay fisheries found around the west. This is my number one pattern, ace in the hole, numero uno, big cheese fly pattern whenever there are big trout around. Period.

Not only is this fly good for trout, but when tied in a variety of colors; brown, blue, purple, red, etc., it is my favorite smallmouth bass fly too.

For trout, this fly should be fished very slowly along the bottom, in a "leech like" fashion.

Hook: Daiichi 1750, sizes 4-8
Thread: Black monocord
Tail: Black marabou
Body: Black Estaz
Overbody: Black bunny strip (Matuka style)
Hackle: Dyed black pheasant rump

Step 1: Secure marabou to hook as shown. Leave a 6-inch piece of tying thread at the butt of the fly.

Step 2: Tie in a 4-inch piece of black Estaz.

Step 3: Wind Estaz forward to form the body.

Step 4: Tie in a piece of black bunny strip as shown.

Step 5: With wet fingers pull the hair upright as shown.

Step 6: Weave the tying thread left at the butt of the fly through the hair, securing the bunny strip "Matuka style".

Step 7: Tie in a dyed black pheasant rump feather in front of the secured bunny strip.

Step 8: Wind the rump feather 2 turns.

Step 9: Finish head and cement to complete the Night Leech.

Leech Yarn Leech

This is another simple, effective leech pattern by Clifford Stringer. This fly is tied entirely of Leech Yarn. It can be tied in a variety of colors, with blacks, olives and browns the most practical.

Hook: Daiichi 2220, sizes 2-14
Thread: Match body color
Body: Leech yarn.

Tying Steps
Step 1: Secure thread to hook and tie in a small bunch of Leech Yarn at the bend of the hook.

Step 2: Continue tying in small bunches of yarn up the hook shank until you reach the eye of the hook.
Step 3: Finish head and cement to complete the Leech Yarn Leech.

Bunny Leech

It was during my first trip to Oregon's Grindstone Lake (before it was even called Grindstone Lake) that I first used the Bunny Leech. When we arrived, Brian O'Keefe made the comment, "I like fishing a lake where you only need one fly." The Bunny Leech produced enough 7-pound trout that day to make me a believer. You can bet I always have a few of these critters in my lake box at all times.

The Bunny Leech is a traditional "big fish" leech pattern widely used across the west, and rightly so—it catches a lot of trout. This fly has plenty of movement, is easy to tie, and should be in every lake fly fisher's fly box.

As with most leech imitations, this fly should be fished slowly along the bottom, using whatever line it takes to accomplish this.

Hook: Daiichi 2421, size 4
Thread: Black monocord
Tail: Black bunny strip and 4 strands of red Krystal Flash
Body: Black bunny strip

Tying Steps
Step 1: Secure a piece of bunny strip, extending past the bend of the hook the length of the hook shank.
Step 2: Tie in 4 strands of Krystal Flash extending to the length of the

bunny strip to complete the tail.
Step 3: Tie in a long strip of bunny strip and wind forward to form the body.
Step 4: Finish head and cement to complete the Bunny Leech.

Bead Egg

Boy, if you had a hard time with the San Juan Worm (page 22), you will definitely have a tough time with this one— the Single Egg. But in Alaska, or anyplace where trout are feeding on salmon roe, this fly is simply the best you can use and, I use the term "fly" loosely.

All this is, is an egg-colored bead tied to a hook. Colors vary due to species of salmon egg, age, etc., and the experienced "Alaskan" angler will go prepared with a variety of sizes and colors.

Many anglers simply slide a bead up the leader and tie on a single hook. I tie my beads directly to the hook, at least, giving myself the illusion that I tied a fly. If it bothers you, don't do it. But if you are not stuck on the "if you

don't fish a dry fly you're not a fly fisherman mentality" and if you're in Alaska and you want to catch big rainbows...use a bead fly!

Hook: Daiichi: 1190 or 1530, size 12 or 14
Thread: Monofilament, 1X is adequate

Egg: Bead (various colors)

Tying Steps
Step 1: Secure monofilament to hook.

Step 2: Pass monofilament through hole in bead, whip finish and cement with Super Glue.

Crayfish

Like the sculpin, crayfish are major food items for large trout. They can be found in most freshwater.

I was once told that trout won't actively pursue crayfish with their pinchers in the defense position (like most patterns on the market) but will chase down fleeing crayfish. I don't know if this is true or not, but when a friend showed me his fleeing crayfish pattern I started tying them, and trout seem to love them.

Hook: Daiichi 1750, sizes 4-10
Weight: A few turns of lead wire near eye of hook
Thread: Copper 3/0
Antenna: Ring-necked pheasant copper body feather, 2 strands of gold
    Flashabou and 2 brown hackle stems
Underbody: Rust Mohair Plus dubbing, or Antron

Overbody: Copper Angel Hair
Pinchers: Ring-necked pheasant
    copper body feathers
Eyes: Mono Eyes (or melt your own
    50lb. monofilament)
Shellback: Copper Swiss straw
Rib: Gold wire

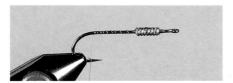

Step 1: Wind lead a few turns near the eye of the hook as shown.

Step 2: Tie in a ring-necked body feather and 2 strands of Flashabou as shown.

Step 3: Wind on a small amount of dubbing as shown. This will make the antennae stand out.

Step 4: Strip the fibers from a brown hackle and tie in the stems as shown.

Step 5: Trim off excess from hackles to finish the antennae.

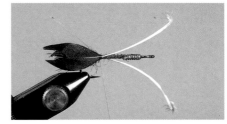

Step 6: Prior to tying on the pinchers, coat the 2 pheasant feathers with Dave's Flexament, and let dry. Cut a "pincher shape" in the feathers and secure, one on each side of the hook as shown.

Step 7: Tie in the Mono Eyes using a figure-eight motion of the tying thread.

Step 8: Tie in a piece of gold wire just behind the eyes.

Step 9: Dub on an underbody of Antron, Mohair Plus, or any appropriately colored dubbing material.

Step 10: Dub on the overbody of Angel Hair.

Step 11: With the copper wire, secure a piece of copper Swiss straw behind the eyes, and segment forward to the eye of the hook.

Step 12: Whip finish thread and cement. Pick out Angel Hair fibers with dubbing teaser or bodkin to complete the Crayfish.

Chickabou Sculpin

Sculpins are a favorite food of big trout. Big sculpin imitations catch big trout.

The sculpin imitation is my first choice when fishing streamers in moving water for trout. It should be fished along the bottom, and retrieved in short, jerky, minnow-like movements to imitate the naturals.

When Hoffman Hackles started marketing Chickabou/ soft hackle patches I found all sorts of uses for them. One of my favorite flies, a result of playing with these feathers is my Chickabou Sculpin. A sculpin tied of these feathers, simply moves and undulates better than more conventional imitations.

Hook: Daiichi 2370, size 2-10
Thread: Brown
Body: Tan Leech Yarn or mohair, then red
Wing/tail: 4 soft hackle feathers from Chickabou patch

Ribbing: Oval gold tinsel
Pectoral Fins: Soft hackle feathers from Chickabou patch
Hackle: Several soft hackle feathers from Chickabou patch

Step 1: Secure a piece of oval gold tinsel to the hook shank and then wind on a body of tan Leech Yarn 3/4 the way up the hook shank.

Step 2: Wind on red Leech Yarn as shown.

Step 3: Select 4 soft-hackle feathers from Chickabou Patch, place 2 together on each side and meld into one with your fingers. Secure in front of the body.

Step 4: Using the oval tinsel, secure the wing "Matuka-style" along the back of the fly.

Step 5: Tie in a soft-hackle tip (curved side out) on each side as shown, to form the pectoral fins.

Step 6: Tie in soft-hackle feathers and wind forward. This may take several feathers, depending on the size of hook. Finish head and cement to complete the Chickabou Sculpin

Trout-Sized Wiggle Bug

When things get so slow I can't buy a fish I often go for a Wiggle Bug. I don't know why I don't grab one sooner, because they nearly always produce. This fly wiggles, dives, wobbles and causes a commotion you have to see to believe.

The Wiggle Bug was designed by Larry Tullis, and has been used effectively all over the world for over 60 species of fish. The trout-sized Wiggle Bug, with the appropriate dressing, color and size can imitate everything from damselfly nymphs to baitfish, crayfish and leeches.

My favorite colors of Wiggle Bugs for trout are black, yellow and olive. The Wiggle Bug can be fished on any line, and will dive down on a slow retrieve. Bodies and complete instructions on tying Wiggle Bugs can be

ordered directly from Larry Tullis at 722 W. 400 South, Orem, Utah 84058 • flyfishlarry@msn.com.

Hook: Daiichi 2461, size 4 or 6
Tail: Black marabou, a few strands of black Krystal Flash

Underbody: Black chenille
Overbody: Black Wiggle Bug foam
Eyes: Painted on

Tying Steps
(See step-by-step photos of the Wiggle Bug in the Salmon section and apply to the trout-sized bug)

Clouser Minnow, Golden Shiner

The Clouser Minnow is one of those streamer patterns that will take large fish everywhere. The Golden Shiner Clouser is one of my very favorites during fall for big brown trout. Casting this pattern to the banks of a stream and swiftly stripping it back will account for some aggressive strikes from the largest of the trout available. During the cover of darkness, this fly is lethal!

Hook: Daiichi 2546, sizes 2/0-6
Thread: Brown, 6/0
Eyes: Lead, dark red with black pupils
Wing: White bucktail on top, with tan bucktail and gold Krystal Flash underneath

Tying Steps
Step 1: Secure a pair of pre-painted dumbell eyes
Step 2: Tie in a length of white bucktail along the hook shank, securing up to the eyes, and then tie down in front of the eyes.

Step 3: Secure several strands of Krystal Flash on the bottom of the hook shank.
Step 4: Tie in a length of tan bucktail over the Krystal Flash, finish head and cement to complete the Clouser Minnow Golden Shiner.

Foam Hornet

There are times during the fall when hornets are found in large numbers around lakes and streams. When trout have the opportunity, they don't hesitate to eat them for lunch. This is a high-floating effective pattern whenever this is the case.

Hook: Daiichi 1280, size 10
Thread: Black monocord
Legs: Rubber leg material
Body: Yellow foam

Step 1: Cover the hook shank with tying thread and secure a strip of three attached, or separate strands of leg material.

Step 2: With a Sharpie permanent marker draw stripes and eyes on a piece of precut foam and attach to the hook behind the eyes as shown.

Step 3: Secure the foam well, and separate the rubber legs with a bodkin if necessary, and whip finish.

Step 4: Coat the entire body with a hard head cement to complete the Foam Hornet.

Steelhead

Steelhead are one of the most coveted game fish to the Northwest fly fisher. These anadromous rainbows, once plentiful in nearly every Northwest water with salt access, have suffered greatly over the years. Their numbers have been greatly reduced by a variety of things; poor logging practices, pollution, over-harvest, gillnets and, of course, the dams. Still, there is a following of dedicated fly-tossers for these magnificent fish. It is a passion hard to describe.

Sometimes hours, even days pass between hook-ups. Cold, soggy weather, numb fingers, and frozen rod guides are all a part of winter steelheading. Some say, a numb brain also helps. But just when you start to question the true worth of it all, you hook into a fish. Those countless days of frozen toes and casting practice are forgotten in an instant.

Summer steelheading is a different thing. Mild Northwest weather, water flows more suitable to the fly fisher and, a host of first-class waters make summer steelhead a more reasonable quarry.

There are still those who feel that it is too hard, or even impossible, to catch steelhead on flies. To that I say, bunk! A steelhead will take a fly just as readily as it will take any artificial, if that fly passes in front of a willing fish. This is where I think many would-be steelhead fly fishers, especially winter steelheaders, fail—they don't get their offering in front of the fish.

Steelhead fly tying patterns and new materials have come a long way since those early steelheading pioneers like Ralph Wahl and Enos Bradner first explored the undammed and generous waters of the Northwest. Nowadays, there are a plethora of patterns available.

I have never been one too convinced that particular patterns make that much difference when it comes to steelheading success. I really feel it's more important to properly place a fly in front of a fish's face. I do feel, however, that size and color are factors at times, when it comes to triggering a strike.

Tying steelhead flies is largely a personal thing. Every steelhead fly fisher has his or her own favorites. In this section I share with you some of my most-often-used steelhead patterns. These are the flies that I go for first whenever I am summer or winter steelheading. They are the patterns you would see if you looked into my steelhead boxes.

Red Butt Skunk

The Skunk has probably accounted for more steelhead than any other summer steelhead pattern. Why? Besides the fact that it is a very good fly, it is probably the most know and widely used summer steelhead fly ever designed.

After the original tie with a solid black body, came variations. Two of the most popular variations are the Green Butt Skunk and the Red Butt Skunk. The only difference is the butt of the fly, which, can really be any color that you wish. The original was also tied with chenille, but any body material you choose can be used.

The Red Butt Skunk is my personal favorite. I especially like this pattern sparsely tied in smaller

sizes, and fished during the heat of summer when streams are low and clear. A floating line and the down-and-across approach is all you need.

Hook: Daiichi 2441, sizes 2-8
Thread: Black
Tail: Scarlet hackle fibers
Butt: Red Frostbite, dubbing, or chenille
Body: Black Frostbite, dubbing, or chennile
Rib: Silver tinsel or Mylar

Hackle: Black
Wing: White polar bear or calf tail

Tying Steps
Step 1: Tie in a tail of scarlet hackle fibers.
Step 2: Wind on a butt of red

Frostbite and then tie in the tinsel and black frostbite, and wind forward.
Step 3: Wind on the hackle 2 or 3 turns.
Step 4: Tie in the wing, finish head and cement to complete the Red Butt Skunk.

Guinea & Black

This is another of my favorite low-water summer steelhead patterns. Its low profile lets it sink easily and the guinea feather provides good movement.

Hook: Daiichi 2441, sizes 4-8
Thread: Red
Tail: Guinea feather fibers
Body: Black Frostbite, floss, or dubbing
Hackle: Natural guinea feather
Wing: White calf tail or polar bear

Tying Steps
Step 1: Tie in a tail of guinea feather fibers.
Step 2: Wind on a body of black Frostbite, floss, or dubbing.
Step 3: Tie in a guinea feather and

wind 2 turns.
Step 4: Secure a small wing of calf tail or polar bear, whip finish and cement to complete the Guinea & Black.

Red Squirrel Frostbite

This is another of my low, clear-water summer steelhead patterns that has become a favorite over the years. Like the Skunk, I mostly tie this fly in small sizes, and with a body of Frostbite.

Hook: Daiichi 1241, sizes 4-8
Thread: Black
Tail: Black hackle fibers
Tag: Silver tinsel
Body: Red Frostbite
Rib: Silver tinsel
Hackle: Black

Wing: Red squirrel tail

Tying Steps
Step 1: Tie in a tag of silver tinsel and then tie in the tail.
Step 2: Wind on a body of red

Frostbite and rib with silver tinsel.
Step 3: Secure a black hackle and wind 3 turns, securing beard style.
Step 4: Tie in the wing, finish head and cement to complete the Red Squirrel Frostbite.

Seal & Polar

Don't panic. If you can't get your hands on seal dubbing and polar bear hair you can still tie this fly. Simply substitute the seal body with your favorite dubbing and the polar bear wing with calf tail.

I have found this color combination effective, and have hooked steelhead under extremely low and clear water conditions.

Hook: 2441, sizes 2-8
Thread: Black
Tag: Gold tinsel
Body: Chartreuse and orange dubbing
Ribbing: Gold tinsel
Hackle: Black

Wing: White polar bear or calf tail
Eye: Jungle cock

Tying Steps
Step 1: Wind on a tag of gold tinsel, leaving a piece of tinsel to be used for the rib.
Step 2: Dub on the body in proportions as seen in the finished fly and rib with the tinsel.
Step 3: Tie in a black hackle and wind beard-style.
Step 4: Secure the wing, tie in a jungle cock feather for the eye, finish head and cement to complete the Seal & Polar.

Teeny Nymph

There is not a whole lot to this little fly but it sure catches its share of summer steelhead. Made of nothing more than ring-necked pheasant center tail fibers, this little fly can be tied in a variety of dyed colors, and has taken several species of fish. My favorite colors for steelhead are brown, black, orange and chartreuse.

Hook: Daiichi 1710, sizes 2- 10
Thread: Black
Body: Ring-necked pheasant center tail fibers
Legs: Tips of pheasant center tail fibers

Tying Steps
Step 1: Tie in pheasant tail fibers and wind forward. Add a second batch of fibers if need be to completely cover the hook.

Step 2: At the head, bend back the tips of the tail fibers and secure as seen on the finished fly. Finish head and cement to complete the Teeny Nymph.

SLF Fall Favorite

The Fall Favorite was traditionally tied with a polar bear wing. When the new fiber, SLF came along I began tying this and several other similar flies substituting the SLF for the polar bear or other wing material. SLF has a sheen very much like natural polar bear.

The Fall Favorite is a good pattern on bright days, fished on a floating line using the down-and-across approach.

Hook: Daiichi 2050, size 1 1/2
Thread: Black
Body: Silver Braid or Mylar
Wing: Orange SLF Hanks
Hackle: Red saddle

Tying Steps
Step 1: Wind on a body of silver Braid or Mylar.
Step 2: Wind a red hackle 2 or 3 turns and secure "beard style".

Step 3: Tie in a wing of orange SLF Hanks, finish head and cement to complete the SLF Fall Favorite.

Skykomish Sunrise

The first steelhead I ever took on a "standard" pattern was taken on a Skykomish Sunrise. To this day, when I go for a bright pattern, I often reach for this fly.

This pattern is fished using the basic down-and-across method. For winter fishing I most often use a heavy sinking-tip or shooting-head and fish it deep. When after summer steelhead I use sparsely dressed Skykomish Sunrises on a floating line.

Hook: Daiichi 2441, size 2/0-8
Thread: Black
Tail: Mixed yellow and red hackle fibers
Body: Red chenille
Rib: Oval silver tinsel
Hackle: 1 yellow and 1 red hackle
Wing: White calf tail or polar bear

Step 1: Tie in a mixture of yellow and red hackle fibers for the tail.

Step 2: Secure a piece of oval silver tinsel and a piece of red chenille. Wind chenille forward to form the body.

Step 3: Wind tinsel forward and secure.

Step 4: Tie in 1 red and 1 yellow hackle.

Step 5: Wind both hackles 2 or 3 turns and secure.

Step 6: Tie in a small wing of white calf tail or polar bear.

Step 7: Finish head and cement to complete the Skykomish Sunrise.

Hohbo

A few years back this pattern quickly became one of my favorite winter steelhead flies. That happens, whenever you catch a fish, or see a fish caught on any fly. While writing the *Steelhead River Journal: The Hoh*, I witnessed my friend Herb Jacobsen catch a fish on a similar pattern. I began tying my version, and since I was spending so much time on the Hoh River working on the book, this fly somehow got dubbed the Hohbo.

Hook: Daiichi 2441, sizes 2/0-4
Thread: Pink
Body: Black Lite Brite (or any sparkle dubbing)

Hackle: Black Spey
Wing/tail: Black bunny strip

Step 1: Dub on a body, leaving a piece of tying thread at the butt of the fly for later use.

Step 2: Cut a piece of rabbit strip to length and tie in at the head as shown.

Step 3: Secure the bunny strip "Matuka-style" with the thread left at the butt of the fly.

Step 4: Tie in a Spey hackle by the tip.

Step 5: Wind hackle 2 turns and secure.

Step 6: Finish head and cement to complete the Hohbo.

Gray Squirrel Purple

One of my favorite "purple" patterns, the Gray Squirrel Purple combines the effectiveness of squirrel tail with the time proven purple color—one of the best for steelhead.

Hook: Daiichi 2441, sizes 2/0-8
Thread: Black
Tail: Gray squirrel tail and a few strands of pink Krystal Flash
Body: Purple chenille
Ribbing: Silver braid
Wing: Gray squirrel tail and a few strands of pink Krystal Flash
Hackle: Purple

Tying Steps
Step 1: Tie in a tail of gray squirrel tail and Krystal Flash.
Step 2: Wind on the body of purple chenille and rib with braid.
Step 3: Tie in a purple hackle and wind on beard-style.
Step 4: Tie in the wing of gray squirrel and Krystal Flash, finish head and cement to complete the Gray Squirrel Purple.

Purple Spey

Spey-type flies have become increasingly popular for summer steelhead fishing. These classic looking patterns sink well and are very effective when fished down-and-across. I especially like fishing them over tailouts.

Some Speys, following the Atlantic salmon tradition, are very elaborate. My favorite though, is this simple Purple Spey—easy to tie—and effective.

Hook: Daiichi 2050, size 1 1/2
Thread: Pink
Body: Purple chenille

Rib: Oval silver tinsel
Hackle: Purple Spey

Step 1: Tie in a piece of oval silver tinsel and a piece of purple chenille.

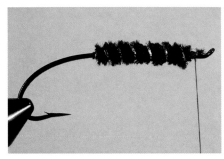

Step 2: Wind chenille forward and rib with the silver tinsel.

Step 3: Strip the fibers off one side of the Spey feather and secure to the hook by the tip as shown.

Step 4: Wind hackle 2 or 3 turns and secure.

Step 5: Finish head and cement to complete the Purple Spey.

Shim's Steelhead/Salmon Dazzel Leech

Like the trout-sized Dazzel Leech, Shim's Steelhead/Salmon Dazzel Leech works its wonders on the steelies just as the smaller version does on the trout. It can be tied in your favorite colors—for steelhead, mine's purple.

Hook: Shim's recommendation—
Gamakatsu L11S-3H, size 8
Thread: Black
Tail & Wing: Angler's Choice Dazzel
Dubbing in purple fuchsia
Bead: 3/16 inch.

Tying Steps
Step 1: Pinch the barb on the hook and slide the bead up to the head.
Step 2: Tie in a tail of Dazzel Dubbing.
Step 3: Loosely dub Dazzel Dubbing up the hook shank forming the body.

Step 4: Tie in a wing of Dazzel Dubbing, melding all the fibers from the tail, body and wing together with your fingers. Pick additional fibers out with a bodkin or dubbing teaser. Whip-finish behind the bead and cement to complete.

Hot Stuff

I spend a lot of time at the tying bench experimenting with materials, combining colors and styles, constantly putting new and different materials together for my steelhead flies. Rarely do I tie many flies the same way twice. If I tie something I like I will usually tie a dozen or so, and maybe never tie it again—at least, not exactly the same way.

I don't mind having a box full of flies with no names. The problem is when I catch a fish on one, or somebody borrows one and asks what it's called. I usually just say that it doesn't have a name. When a fly does get a name it's usually because my fishing partner called for another one and threw a name on it. That's the case with the Hot Stuff. A friend hooked and lost a steelhead on one and said, "give me another one of those flies. It was hot stuff!" The name stuck.

Hook: Daiichi 2151, sizes 1-10
Thread: Black
Body: Rear 2/3 silver braid. Front 1/3 your favorite orange dubbing
Ribbing: Oval silver tinsel
Hackle: Natural mallard flank

Wing: Olive dyed mallard flank

Tying Steps
Step 1: Wind on the silver braid and ribbing up the rear 2/3 of the hook shank. Then dub the front 1/3 with your favorite dubbing.
Step 2: Tie in a mallard flank feather and wind 2 or 3 turns.
Step 3: Secure a wing of olive mallard flank, finish head and cement to complete the Hot Stuff.

Nasty Mallard

This is one of my favorite patterns for both summer and winter fish. It has everything I like in a steelhead fly—flash, movement, and a great color combination. I tie it in a variety of sizes—as large as size 1 for winter fish and as small as size 10 for summer fish. Fish it using a down-and-across approach.

Hook: Daiichi 2151, sizes 1-10
Thread: Black
Body: Rear 2/3 gold braid. Front 1/3 River Green Lite Brite
Rib: Oval gold tinsel
Hackle: Black Spey

Wing: Natural mallard flank feather

Tying Steps
Step 1: Wind on the rear portion of the body and the ribbing.
Step 2: Loosely dub on the front portion of the body.
Step 3: Wind a black Spey hackle 2 turns.
Step 4: Secure a wing of natural mallard flank, finish head and cement to complete the Nasty Mallard.

Herb's Hoh Fly

While working on my River Journal on Washington's Hoh River, I fished quite a bit with Herb Jacobson, a guide who, at the time, guided on the Olympic Peninsula. One of his favorite flies for the Hoh River is this pattern. When I asked what it was called his response was, "It doesn't have a name." So, I dubbed it "Herb's Hoh Fly."

Hook: Alec Jackson Spey Hook 1 1/2 nickle, or TMC 7999, sizes 2/0-8
Thread: Black
Body: Rear half: chartreuse floss Front half: chartreuse dubbing
Ribbing: Oval silver tinsel
Tail: Purple saddle hackle fibers

Wing: Arctic fox tail
Collar: Purple saddle hackle

Tying Steps
Step 1: Tie in the tail, and secure a piece of floss and the ribbing material.
Step 2: Wind floss forward 1/2 way up the hook. Dub the remaining 1/2, and wind on the ribbing.
Step 3: Tie in a purple saddle hackle and wind 2 or 3 turns. Secure most of the fibers underneath the hook beard-style.
Step 4: Tie in the wing, finish head and cement to complete Herb's Hoh Fly.

Material Girl

This is another favorite steelhead fly of Herb Jacobson for the steelhead rivers of the Olympic Peninsula. But my guess is that this fly will work anywhere steelhead are found!

Hook: Alec Jackson Spey 1 1/2 or TMC 7999 sizes 8-2/0
Thread: Black
Tail: Red calf tail or hackle fibers
Body: Rear half: hot pink floss
    Front half: purple dubbing
Wing: Red calf tail

Hackle: Black saddle hackle

Tying Steps
Step 1: Tie in the tail.
Step 2: Wind on the floss for the rear 1/2 of the body and secure. Coat with clear fingernail polish.

Step 3: Dub on the front 1/2 of the body.
Step 4: Tie in a saddle hackle and wind 2 or 3 turns. Tie in the wing, finish head and cement to complete the Material Girl.

Mega Bugger

The Woolly Bugger being the incredible fly it is, inevitably found it's way into the boxes of steelhead fly fishers. It works for both summer and winter fish, and can be tied in a variety of colors and using a variety of materials. The Mega Bugger is my standard for winter fish.

Hook: Daiichi 2441, sizes 2/0 or 1/0
Thread: Black
Tail: Black marabou
Body: Large purple chenille
Hackle: Black saddle

Tying Steps
Step 1: Tie in a tail of 3 marabou tips.
Step 2: Secure a short piece of purple chenille and wind forward a few turns. Then tie in a hackle and wind

3 turns. Repeat this process up the body so there are a total of 4 hackles wound as seen in the finished fly. Finish head and cement to complete the Mega Bugger.

Prawn

Several variations of Prawn patterns are on the market, as the prawn is a popular fly for steelhead, especially in coastal rivers. This fly is fished with the standard down-and-across approach, and swung through steelhead holding water.

I tied this version of the prawn after recalling one that I saw somewhere and particularly liked. Of course, a variety of synthetic materials can be substituted in the tying of this pattern.

Hook: Daiichi 2441, size 2/0
Thread: Maroon, orange or copper
Body: Orange Krystal Chenille or Estaz
Tail: Orange Silky Fibers
Antennae: Copper Krystal Flash
Eyes: Mono Eyes
Carapace: Copper Krystal Flash

Hackle: Orange schlappen, palmered

Tying Steps
Step 1: Secure the tail and antennae to extend past the bend 1 1/2 times the hook shank length.
Step 2: Secure the Krystal Flash and Krystal Chenille.

Step 3: Tie on the Mono Eyes with a figure-eight motion of the tread.
Step 4: Wind the chenille forward and secure behind the eyes.
Step 5: Tie in a Schlappin feather by the tip, and finish winding on the body.
Step 6: Pull the Krystal Flash forward and secure. Finish head and cement to complete the Prawn.

Steelhead Bead Fly

Okay, if this looks too much like an Okie Drifter to you—better turn the page. But if you are looking for a clear-water pattern that sinks like a rock and seems to work when most others fail—better tie up a few of these for both your summer and winter box.

Fish this fly "dead drift" on a floating line using the basic, short-line nymphing technique. In other words, fish it the same as you would if using drift tackle.

Hook: Daiichi 2250, size 2
Thread: Orange
Body: Orange bead
Tail: 1 light orange and 1 dark orange marabou feather

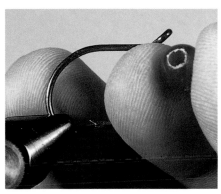

Step 1: Select an appropriate sized bead. You may need to drill the hole larger so that it will slide over the hook shank.

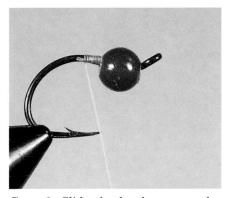

Step 2: Slide the bead up over the hook shank and secure the tying thread as shown.

Step 3: Tie in the tips of the 2 marabou feathers.

Step 4: Secure a small bunch of orange Krystal Flash on top of the marabou.

Step 5: Wind the tying thread to a thickness so that the bead barely slides over.

Step 6: Slide bead over the top of the built up thread body and wind the tying thread in front of the bead so it doesn't slip.

Step 7: Whip finish and cement the entire thread area and the bead to complete the Steelhead Bead Fly.

Sandshrimp

I have caught more winter steelhead on this pattern than on any other winter steelhead fly I have used. But then, I use this fly more than any other, and that's often the case with steelheaders. If they catch a fish on any given fly, it becomes a favorite, and inevitably gets used more than other patterns, ultimately catching more fish.

Sandshrimp (ghost shrimp) are a favorite bait among steelheaders. One day at the tying bench I came up with this imitation and began using it in Northwest streams. The results were most favorable.

I fish this fly in very much the same manner the drifters fish their live bait. Using a floating line and long leader (9 to 12 feet) I dead drift this pattern through likely holding water; around rocks, along logs, banks, pools—basically anywhere I can identify as good holding water. Following the line and fly with my rod tip through its drift, I keep a close eye on my line and leader. If anything out of the ordinary happens—line stops, twitches, etc.—I set the hook.

Hook: Daiichi 2151, size 1
Thread: Orange monocord
Weight: Medium lead wire
Body: Orange Estaz
Hackle: Brown schlappen
Shellback and tail: Orange Swiss straw, then orange Krystal Flash
Rib: Orange tying thread

Step 1: Wind on lead wire as shown.

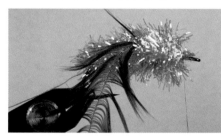

Step 2: Secure lead wire with tying thread. Tie in a piece of Estaz, leaving a section of tying thread at the butt to be used later for the ribbing.

Step 3: Wind body forward, 1/2 the way up the hook as shown and secure.

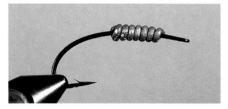

Step 4: Tie in a Schlappen feather by the tip.

Step 5: Tie in more Estaz and finish winding on the body.

Step 6: Wind hackle forward and secure.

Step 7: Tie in a piece of orange Estaz at the head as shown.

Step 8: Secure a small bunch of Krystal Flash over the Swiss straw as shown.

Step 9: Using the thread left at the butt, secure the shellback in segments, leaving one large segment (the hackled segment).

Step 10: Trim excess material at head and cut the tail down as shown.

Step 11: Finish head and cement to complete the Sandshrimp.

Yarn Fly

This is another fly that I dead-drift using the basic, short-line nymphing technique. Like the Sandshrimp, this fly should be drifted along structure, or anyplace you expect a steelhead to be holding. It is a great pattern to use when the bottom keeps stealing your fly—it's easy and quick to tie.

Hook: Daiichi 2550, size 2 or 4
Thread: Pink, orange, red, chartreuse (match yarn color)
Yarn: Glo Bug Yarn
Flash: Holographic Flash
Eyes: Brass

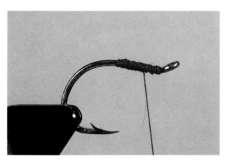

Step 1: Secure thread to hook and wind on a base.

Step 2: Tie in a tuft of yarn as shown.

Step 3: Tie in a few strands of Holographic Flash. Trim yarn and flash to length as shown.

Step 4: Tie in a set of brass eyes using a figure-eight motion of the tying thread.

Step 5: Coat the thread with a few coats of head cement to complete the Yarn Fly.

Super Floss Jig

Over the past few years jig fishing for steelhead has become very popular. It is a very effective way to take both summer and winter steelhead.

This jig/fly combines a purple body with the movement of Super Floss used for the legs. It is great for prospecting deep pools or drifting along structure.

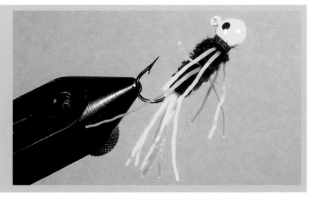

Hook: Standard jig hook painted chartreuse
Eyes: Painted on
Thread: Pink
Tail: Chartreuse Super Floss
Body: Purple chenille
Legs: Chartreuse Super Floss

Tying Steps
Step 1: Paint your jig head complete with eye, or buy a pre-painted jig.
Step 2: Tie in several strands of Super Floss for the tail.
Step 3: Secure chenille to hook and wind forward. Tie in Super Floss legs along the way as seen in the finished jig.
Step 4: Whip finish behind the head and cement to complete the Super Floss Jig.

Glue Gun Egg

A quick and nifty way to make egg patterns is to use a hot glue gun. Glue sticks come in a variety of egg colors. When these eggs are in the water they look just like the real thing. What self-respecting steelhead could possibly refuse? It takes some practice to make these eggs, but once you get it down you can turn out five dozen an hour.

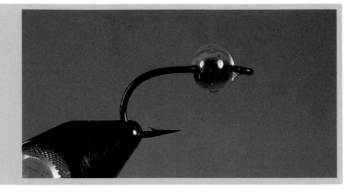

Hook: Daiichi 2451, size 2 or 4
Egg: Clear hot glue over red hot glue

Tying Steps
Step 1: Place a small dab of red hot glue to the hook shank and dip in a bowl of cold water to set.
Step 2: Quickly surround the hardened red glue with clear or orange hot glue, spinning the hook to form the glue in a round egg shape and size. When the desired shape is obtained, immediately dip the egg in a bowl of cold water to set. You now have a finished Glue Gun Egg.

Double Egg

Like the single Glue Gun Egg, the Double Egg is easy to make, and very effective for steelhead and salmon. With the added marabou, this fly looks very realistic when in the water.

Hook: Daiichi 2441, size 4
Thread: White
Body: Orange or red hot glue
Collar: White marabou

Tying Steps:
Step 1: Follow the steps for the single Glue Gun Egg to form the two eggs on the hook shank.
Step 2: Secure a marabou plume and wind 2 or 3 turns, whip finish and cement to complete the Double Egg.

Estaz Comet

This is a variation of the standard Comet that has a lot of movement and is effective for both summer and winter steelhead. It also takes its share of sea-run cutthroat when tied in smaller sizes.

Hook: Daiichi 2441, size 10-2/0
Tail: Silky Fibers
Body: Purple Estaz
Hackle: Purple hen hackle or Chickabou

Tying Steps
Step 1: Secure the tail, which is approximately the length of the hook shank.
Step 2: Tie in bead-chain eyes using a figure-eight motion of the tying thread.
Step 3: Wind on a body of Estaz
Step 4: Tie on and wind a long soft hackle or Chickabou feather several turns.
Step 5: Finish head and cement to complete the Estaz Comet.

Steelhead Leech

This one is about as simple as they get—yet is a very effective pattern for steelhead. It can be tied in a variety of colors, but for steelhead, black or purple are my favorites. Try pink, orange or chartreuse for salmon. This fly works well when dead-drifted, as well as when swung with the down-and-across approach.

Hook: X510, size 4
Thread: Black (match wing/tail color
Wing/tail: 2-inch piece of black rabbit strip

Eyes: Spirit River I-Balz

Tying Steps
Step 1: Secure eyes using a figure-eight motion of the tying thread.
Step 2: Tie in the rabbit strip, whip finish and cement, to complete the Steelhead Leech.

Purple Conehead

This is another of those patterns that I consistently reach for when winter steelheading. It has all the components I like in a steelhead fly—color, movement, flash and weight. Of course, it can be tied in several colors, but purple and black are my two favorites.

Hook: Daiichi 2441, size 2/0
Thread: Black
Cone: Gold
Body: Purple Krystal Chenille or Estaz
Tail/wing: Purple bunny strip
Legs: Black rubber leg material
Hackle: Purple schlappen

Tying Steps
Step 1: De-barb the hook and slide a gold cone to the eye.
Step 2: Tie in the body material and wind forward. Leave a piece of tying thread at the butt of the fly.
Step 3: Secure a piece of purple bunny strip behind the cone.
Step 4: With the thread left at the butt, wind forward, weaving the thread through the rabbit hair and tie down the rabbit strip "Matuka-style."
Step 5: Secure 2 strands of rubber leg material behind the cone using a figure-eight motion of the thread, resulting in 2 legs on each side of the body.
Step 6: Tie on and wind a purple schlappen feather 3 turns, whip finish and cement behind the cone to complete the Purple Conehead.

Black & Blue

Like the Purple Conehead, the Black & Blue is one of my favorite winter steelhead patterns. And, like most flies of this type, it can be tied in a variety of colors, using a wide variation of materials.

Hook: Daiich 2441, size 4-2/0
Thread: Black
Eyes: Nickel dumbell
Body: Black Holographic Estaz
Tail/wing/collar: Black bunny strip
Overbody: Blue Flashabou

Tying Steps
Step 1: Secure the eyes using a figure-eight motion of the tying thread.
Step 2: Wind on the body, leaving a piece of tying thread at the butt to secure the wing.
Step 3: Tie in a piece of bunny strip behind the eyes.
Step 4: Secure the bunny at the butt with the length of thread left there, and wind thread forward, weaving through the bunny hair, securing the wing to the body. Tie off behind the eyes. Leave the excess rabbit strip to be used for the hackle.
Step 5: Tie in several strands of blue Flashabou over the bunny strip and trim as seen in the finished fly.
Step 6: With the leftover rabbit strip, wind two turns behind the eyes, whip finish behind the eyes and cement to complete the Blue & Black.

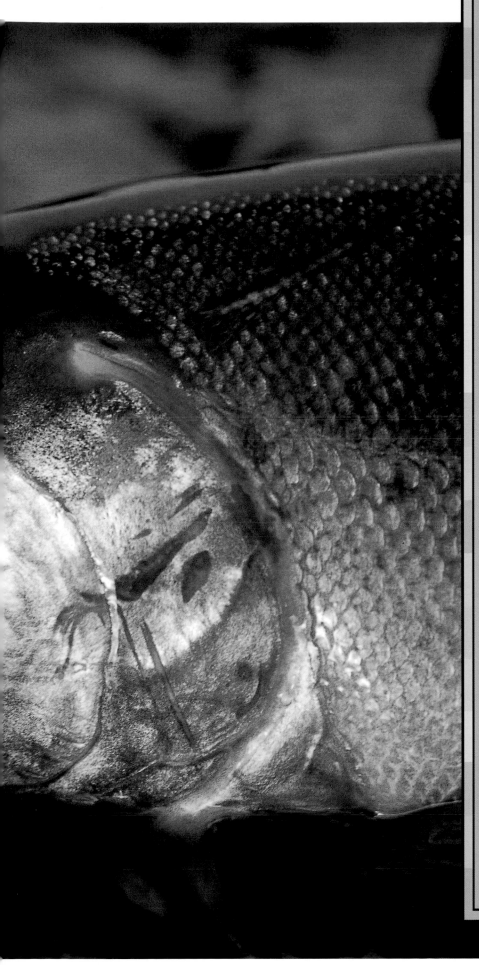

Salmon

Fly fishing for Atlantic salmon is a sport that has been enjoyed since the early days of fly fishing. Fly fishing for Pacific salmon is a fairly new sport by comparison. The ranks of those targeting Pacific salmon with fly rods are still quite low. It is a growing sport however, and each season finds more and more anglers on the water, long-rod in hand. All five species of Pacific salmon can be taken on flies.

Salmon in rivers can be quite moody and persistence is required to get one to strike. This is especially true with hatchery fish which are much harder to take on flies than wild fish. It can be a real test of patience. But at times, the fish come easily, making those dry spells all worthwhile.

The key to fishing for salmon in fresh water with a fly is to place your offering in front of the fish's face repeatedly. Sooner or later you will provoke a strike. The trick is to be able to read the water and know where the fish will be holding. Pools below riffles are a good place to start.

More fly fishers fish for Pacific salmon in fresh water than in salt water. This is simply because of access. Not everyone has a seaworthy boat. However, saltwater angling for salmon is gaining in popularity in the Northwest.

In general, feeding saltwater fish are much easier to fool with a fly than those that have entered fresh water. Their instincts are still telling them to eat, eat, eat. A properly fished fly, I feel, is nearly as productive as bait.

Regardless of where you fish—fresh water, salt water; anyplace along the north Pacific coast where salmon are found—fly rodding for these anadromous giants of the Pacific is an incredible sport, one that gets under your skin once you have tried it.

Tandem Candlefish

When fishing for Pacific salmon in salt water, the wise fly fisher will use imitations of their natural foods. Sometimes salmon, like trout, can be very fussy about just what's on the menu. One of their favorites is the candlefish.

I use this Candlefish pattern for both blind-searching the water and when I find salmon feeding on baitfish. When salmon are aggressively feeding, baitfish will often school in a tight ball pushed near the surface by the charging salmon. A concentration of sea birds feeding on the surface is a good indication that this is happening.

When fishing over a bait ball, cast the Tandem Candlefish right into the school. Let the fly sink several seconds and start an erratic retrieve to mimic the movements of the panicked baitfish.

Hooks: Main hook: long shank, stainless steel, size 2.
  Trailing hook: Standard length, turned-up-eye, stainless, size 2
Thread: White monocord

Wing: White SLF, pearl and light green Krystal Flash, orange Super Hair
Belly: Pearlescent Lite Brite
Eyes: Prismatic adhesive eyes
Head coating: Five-minute epoxy

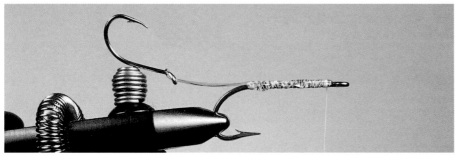

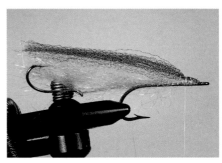

Step 1: Connect the hooks with a piece of 40-pound-test monofilament. To do this, thread the ends of the mono through the eye of the trailing hook and pass the looped end over the bend of the hook below the shank. Pull the mono tight against the eye. Secure the mono to the main hook with the tying thread and coat with Super Glue to form the hook assembly as shown.

Step 2: Secure a bunch of white SLF to the main hook, then the pearl and green Krystal Flash.

Step 3: Tie in the orange Super Hair (or substitute with orange Krystal Flash) along the sides as shown, and secure a small tuft of Lite Brite to the bottom of the hook. Blend all the wing/body materials together with your fingers.

Step 4: Build up the head with the tying thread and secure a pair of prismatic adhesive eyes as shown.

Step 5: Coat the head with five-minute epoxy and rotate until cured to complete the Tandem Candlefish.

Saltwater Baitfish

This general baitfish imitation has proven itself in the open ocean as well as in sheltered marine waters such as Puget Sound and various estuaries up and down the Pacific coast.

Fish this fly anyplace saltwater salmon are feeding on small baitfish. Remember to strip the fly in erratically to mimic the panicked prey.

Hook: Long shank stainless steel, size 2/0
Thread: White monocord
Tail: Golden pheasant neck
Body: Silver braid
Beard: Pearl Lite Brite
Eyes: Pearl adhesive eyes
Wing: White SLF Hanks, then Krystal Flash, then silver Flashabou, then peacock herl

Tying Steps
Step 1: Take two green neck feathers from a golden pheasant skin and secure (dull sides together) to form the tail.
Step 2: Tie in a piece of silver braid and wind on the body.
Step 3: To form the wing, tie in a small bunch of white SLF, then pearl Krystal Flash, then silver Flashabou, then top off with a few strands of peacock herl.
Step 4: Tie in the beard of pearl Lite Brite.
Step 5: Wind on a large head with the tying thread and place an adhesive eye to each side.
Step 6: Coat the head with five-minute epoxy and rotate until set to complete the Saltwater Baitfish.

Herring

Another favorite saltwater food of the salmon is the herring. These large baitfish are the most widely used bait along the coast, and I have found my herring pattern to be very effective for both chinook and coho salmon. This large fly looks very realistic when swimming through the water.

For chinook salmon, I fish this pattern down deep. A 700-grain head is my usual choice. However, for coho, I most often use a 300-grain line, and have even taken aggressive feeders on a full-floating line near the surface.

Hook: Trey Combs Big Game Hook, size 2/0
Thread: White monocord
Body/wing: White SLF Hanks, then pearl Krystal Flash, then blue Krystal Flash, then green Krystal Flash, then peacock Angel Hair
Lateral line: Silver Krystal Flash
Gills: Red SLF Hanks
Throat/bottom of body: Pearl Lite Brite
Eyes: Prismatic stick-on
Head coating: Five-minute epoxy

Tying Steps
Step 1: Secure thread to the hook at the head and build the body of the herring of white SLF Hanks, then pearl Krystal Flash, then blue Krystal Flash, then green Krystal Flash then peacock Angel Hair.
Step 2: Tie in an ample bunch of pearl Lite Brite on the bottom side of the hook to form the bottom of the body.
Step 3: Tie in a small amount of silver Krystal Flash on both sides of the body to form the lateral line. Blend all the body materials together with your fingers to form the body.
Step 4: Tie a small tuft of red SLF Hanks to each side of the fly for the gills.
Step 5: Build up a large head with the tying thread and whip finish. Apply stick-on eyes to each side of the head.
Step 6: Coat the head with five-minute epoxy and rotate until set to complete the Herring.

Tullis Wiggle Bug

Since Larry Tullis created the Wiggle Bug it has been used for such diverse species as steelhead, trout, bass, tarpon, bonefish and a host of other species. My favorite species to target with this fly is Pacific salmon; I have taken chinook, coho, chum and sockeye salmon in rivers with this fly. By nature of its design, the Wiggle Bug swims and dives very much like a hard-bodied plug—an action most fish find irresistible.

The foam used for the body comes in several sizes and colors. You can also paint the bodies to suit your fancy. Just about any tail and body combination can be used. The most common are marabou for the tail and chenille for the body.

The Wiggle Bug will float on a slack line and dive down when retrieved. Experimenting with various lines will give you a feel for the Wiggle Bug's action. It is best fished with a slow, long retrieve.

Wiggle Bug Bodies can now also be found in many fly shops.

Hook: Long shank, stainless, straight-eye, 2/0
Thread: Heavy thread to match body color
Underbody: Large chenille or Estaz
Overbody: Tullis Wiggle Foam
Tail: Marabou (match underbody color), Krystal Flash (match overbody color), and a few strands of Holographic Flash
Eyes: Painted on with fabric, or other, paint

Step 1: Secure a piece of chenille to the hook and wind on the underbody.

Step 2: Place a drop of Super Glue above the body as shown.

Step 3: With a bodkin, punch a hole in the body foam. Start the hole just over the distance of the hook's gape from the front of the diving lip and angle the hole backwards at a 45-degree angle. ***The correct angle is critical for proper action.***

Step 4: Slide the foam over the hook eye as shown.

Step 5: With the tying thread secure the overbody at the butt of the fly. Cut foam so that it extends about 1/4 inch past the point where you tied it down.

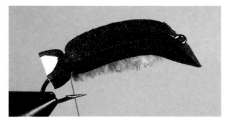

Step 6: With a sharp knife cut a wedge on the top of the foam as shown.

Step 7: Tie in the marabou, Holographic Flash and Krystal Flash to form the tail. Whip finish and cement at the butt. Trim the Holographic Flash and Krystal Flash to the length of the marabou.

Step 8: Paint on eyes with fabric or some other paint to complete the Tullis Wiggle Bug.

Holographic Flash Fly

The Flash Fly has long been a popular Alaskan pattern for salmon. In freshwater rivers and streams, its sparkle is a definite fish attractor and this fly is responsible for a great number of happy stream anglers all along the Pacific coast wherever salmon are found.

I tie the Flash Fly a little more sparsely than the original tie, and I also substitute the Silver Flashabou wing and tail with Holographic Flash.

This fly can be tied in a variety of colors, this is my favorite for coho and chum salmon.

Hook: Daiichi 2151, sizes 1 or 2
Thread: Pink
Tail: Pink Holographic Flash

Body: Green Braid Ribbon
Hackle: Pink saddle
Wing: Brown calf tail, then pink Holographic Flash

Step 1: Tie in a short tail of small Holographic Flash as shown.

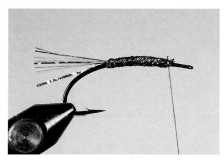

Step 2: Secure a piece of green Braid Ribbon and wind on a body.

Step 3: Tie in a pink saddle hackle by the tip as shown.

Step 4: Wind the hackle two or three turns and secure.

Step 5: Tie in a wing of brown calf tail.

Step 6: Secure the Holographic Flash over the calf tail.

Step 7: Trim Holographic Flash to length of tail, finish head and cement to complete the Holographic Flash Fly.

Sockeye Orange

While Alaska fishing for sockeye salmon this fly outproduced all others. I have since used it at home for coho and chum salmon. This fly sinks fast and the head can be tied in a variety of colors, giving it a different look. My favorite colors for salmon are orange, red and chartreuse.

Hook: Daiichi 2131 or equivalent, sizes 2-4
Thread: Orange monocord (match head color)
Tail: Red squirrel tail
Body: Gold tinsel or Mylar
Wing: Red squirrel tail
Hackle: Orange saddle (match head color)

Head: Orange (or red or chartreuse) chenille
Eyes: Gold bead chain

Step 1: Tie in a tail of red squirrel as shown.

Step 2: Secure a piece of gold Mylar or tinsel and wind on a body.

Step 3: Tie in an orange saddle hackle tip as shown.

Step 4: Wind hackle 2 or 3 turns and secure.

Step 5: Tie in a wing of red squirrel tail.

Step 6: Secure bead-chain eyes using a figure-eight motion of the thread.

Step 7: Tie in a piece of orange chenille and wind forward forming the head.

Step 8: Whip finish at the head and cement to complete the Sockeye Orange.

Chartreuse Egg

The simplest, and possibly most effective, fly for salmon in rivers is the egg pattern. There are many styles of eggs on the market, mine is one of the easiest to tie.

Tie these eggs in a variety of colors; oranges, reds, and my favorite—chartreuse. Fish them dead-drift using the short-line nymphing technique through areas where you know salmon will be holding or moving; chutes, below riffles, etc. Use just enough weight to keep your fly on the bottom and set the hook at the slightest pause in the flies drift.

Hackle: Orange saddle (match head color)
Head: Orange (or red or chartreuse) chenille
Eyes: Gold bead chain

Hook: Daiichi 2550, or any "Octopus" salmon hook, size 2
Body: Glo Bug yarn
Beard: Krystal Flash

Tying Steps
Step 1: Secure thread at the head of the fly and tie in a short piece of Glo Bug yarn.
Step 2: Loop yarn over creating the egg and secure again in the same spot.
Step 3: Tie in a few strands of Krystal Flash as a beard, whip finish head and cement to complete the Chartreuse Egg.

Chumley

When salmon angling in the myriad rivers around the Northwest there is probably no better pattern than this fly, designed by Alaskan guide Jeff Topp. The simple down-and-across approach is the ticket when fishing this pattern, which is especially killer for chum and coho salmon.

Hook: Daiichi 2441, size 2/0
Thread: Pink
Eyes: Nickel dumbell
Body: Pink Cactus Chenille or Estaz
Tail/wing/collar: Pink bunny strip
Overwing: Blue Flashabou

Tying Steps
Step 1: Secure the eyes using a figure-eight motion of the tying thread.
Step 2: Wind on the body, leaving a piece of tying thread at the butt to secure the wing.
Step 3: Tie in a piece of bunny strip behind the eyes.
Step 4: Secure the bunny at the butt with the length of thread left there, and wind thread forward, weaving through the bunny hair, securing the wing to the body. Tie off behind the eyes. Leave the excess rabbit strip to be used for the hackle.
Step 5: Tie in several strands of blue Flashabou over the bunny strip and trim as seen in the finished fly.
Step 6: With the leftover rabbit strip, wind two turns behind the eyes, whip finish behind the eyes and cement to complete the Chumley.

Chartreuse Clouser

One of the best simple flies for saltwater salmon angling is the Clouser Minnow. Most of the time, it is the Chartreuse Clouser that works best for me, although several colors can be used.

Hook: Daiichi 2546, sizes 2-2/0
Thread: Chartreuse
Eyes: Lead, white with black pupils
Wing: White Saltwater Yak Hair on top, chartreuse Yak Hair and Holographic Flash underneath

Tying Steps
Step 1: Secure a pair of pre-painted dumbell eyes.
Step 2: Tie in a length of white Yak Hair along the hook shank, securing up to the eyes, and then tie down in front of the eyes.
Step 3: Secure several strands of Holographic Flash on the bottom of the hook shank.
Step 4: Tie in a length of chartreuse Yak Hair over the Krystal Flash, finish head and cement to complete the Chartreuse Clouser.

Sea-Run Cutthroat

The sea-run cutthroat is found in rivers and streams with salt access from northern California to Prince William Sound in Alaska. This anadromous strain of cutthroat will hit flies with gusto. They are strong, aggressive, beautiful native trout of the Pacific watershed.

Over the years the sea-run cutthroat has had its ups and downs. In some waters they have fallen victim to the ignorance and greed of man, their natural spawning grounds ruined by pollution and poor logging practices. Yet in other waters they are doing fine.

Nearly every river, stream or slough with salt access will host cutthroat as they return from the salt to spawn. Their return usually occurs from mid-summer through the fall. They spawn during winter and return to the salt during early spring.

Sea-run prefer the frog water—slow-moving, leaf-covered areas where you would normally skip if fishing for rainbow or other trout. Root wads and other structure are also good bets when trying to locate these fish.

Saltwater angling for cutthroat is a productive affair at times. Sea-runs can be found in schools feeding in estuaries along shorelines and over oyster beds. A small baitfish pattern usually does the trick here.

Whether fishing for sea-run cutthroat in fresh or salt water, the fly fisher who gets into a school of these little powerhouses is in for a real treat.

Gray Hackle Peacock

Sea-run cutthroat are aggressive, non-selective feeders most of the time. If it moves, it's food. In freshwater fishing, heavily-hackled patterns which impart plenty of movement are the most effective. One of my favorites is the simple Gray Hackle Peacock.

Fish this fly, as with all sea-run flies, along brackish edges, around root wads and in pools. A floating line is all that's usually needed as these fish will charge a great distance to slam a fly.

Hook: Daiichi 1550, sizes 8-14
Thread: Black
Tail: Scarlet hackle fibers
Body: Peacock herl
Hackle: Grizzly hen

Tying Steps
Step 1: Tie in a tail of scarlet hackle fibers.
Step 2: Wind on a body of peacock herl.

Step 3: Secure a soft grizzly hen hackle and wind three or four turns, finish head and cement to complete the Gray Hackle Peacock.

Grizzly King

The Grizzly King is an old wet-fly pattern that long ago found its way into the hands of sea-run cutthroat anglers. It is a very effective fly with a slim profile and sinks well.

Hook: Daiichi 2421, sizes 6-10
Thread: Black
Tail: Scarlet hackle fibers
Body: Green floss
Ribbing: Oval gold or silver tinsel
Hackle: Grizzly hen

Wing: Mallard flank feathers

Tying Steps
Step 1: Tie in a tail of scarlet hackle fibers.
Step 2: Wind on a body of green floss

and rib with oval gold tinsel.
Step 3: Wind a grizzly hen hackle three or four turns.
Step 4: Secure a wing of mallard flank feather fibers, finish head and cement to complete the Grizzly King.

Purple Chick

This is a fly that I originally started tying for steelhead, and it's one that I often use when both sea-run cutthroat and steelhead are present.

Hook: Daiichi 2421, sizes 4-10
Thread: Black
Tail: Pink Chickabou soft hackle.
Body: Purple Frostbite
Ribbing: Flat silver tinsel or Mylar
Hackle: Pink Chickabou soft hackle

Wing: White SLF Hanks

Tying Steps
Step 1: Tie in a tail of Chickabou soft hackle.
Step 2: Wind on a body of purple

Frostbite and rib with tinsel.
Step 3: Wind a Chickabou soft hackle two or three turns.
Step 4: Secure a wing of white SLF Hanks, finish head and cement to complete the Purple Chick.

Spruce Matuka

The Spruce fly has long been a favorite sea-run streamer along the Pacific coast. I prefer to tie this pattern "Matuka-style" with the wing tied down.

Hook: Daiichi 1750, sizes 6-10
Thread: Black
Tail: Peacock sword
Body: Red floss/peacock herl
Wing: Two badger saddle hackles
Rib: Oval gold tinsel
Hackle: Badger

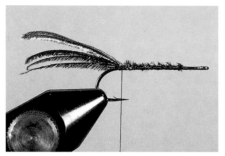

Step 1: Tie in a tail of peacock swords.

Step 2: Tie in a piece of red floss and oval gold tinsel.

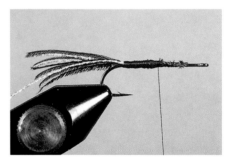

Step 3: Wind floss forward 1/2 way up hook shank.

Step 4: Secure several strands of peacock herl in front of floss.

Step 5: Wind herl forward as shown.

Step 6: Tie in 2 badger saddle hackles.

Step 7: Wind tinsel forward securing hackles Matuka-style.

Step 8: Tie in another badger saddle hackle as shown.

Step 9: Wind hackle two or three turns, finish head and cement to complete the Spruce Matuka.

My Mistake

This fly came about one day while I was tying a batch of Skykomish Sunrise flies. Gabbing with a friend and not paying attention to what I was doing, I left out a few materials and absentmindedly changed some others. The result is My Mistake.

Knowing that sea-run cutthroat are not overly selective, I tied up a few more of this pattern and hit the stream. The rest, as they say, is history and today I always have a few of these flies in my cutthroat box.

Hook: Daiichi 2421, sizes 6-10
Thread: Black
Tail: Scarlet hackle fibers
Body: Red chenille
Ribbing: Oval gold tinsel
Wing: White SLF Hanks

Hackle: Grizzly hen

Tying Steps
Step 1: Tie in a tail of scarlet hackle fibers.
Step 2: Wind on a body of red chenille

and rib with oval gold tinsel.
Step 3: Tie in a grizzly hen hackle and wind three or four turns.
Step 4: Secure a wing of white SLF Hanks, finish head and cement to complete My Mistake.

Gray Hackle Yellow

Another very popular cutthroat pattern, the Gray Hackle Yellow is time proven for these anadromous cutthroat trout of the Pacific coast.

Hook: Daiichi 1550 or 2421, sizes 6-10
Thread: Black
Tail: Scarlet hackle fibers
Body: Yellow chenille or floss
Ribbing: Oval gold tinsel

Hackle: Grizzly hen

Tying Steps
Step 1: Tie in a tail of scarlet hackle fibers.
Step 2: Wind on a body of small

yellow chenille and rib with oval gold tinsel.
Step 3: Tie in a soft hen hackle and wind three or four turns to complete the Gray Hackle Yellow.

Fred's Alevin

This little alevin imitation was created by Fred V. Contaoi, and is one of the best alevin patterns I have ever used. It is effective for virtually every game fish that feeds on the alevin stage of the salmon; rainbows, lake trout, Dolly Varden, arctic char, grayling and sea-run cutthroat trout.

Fish this pattern with the wet-fly swing, imparting an erratic swimming motion and hang on!

Hook: Tiemco 9394, sizes 6 and 8
Thread: 6/0 light pink
Egg sack: 2 beads on size 6, 1 bead on size 8
Body: White marabou
Tail: Tip ends of marabou body
Underwing: Silver or pearl Lite Brite
Midwing: White marabou
Overwing: Peacock or purple Lite Brite

Head: Silicone
Eyes: Silver adhesive stick-on eyes

Tying Steps
Step 1: Slide beads up hook. Tie on a base of thread and anchor far enough from the eye to leave room for the head.
Step 2: Tie in marabou above point of the hook leaving 1/8 inch of the tips for the tail. Then wind remaining

marabou forward to the beads and secure. Trim butt ends of marabou.
Step 3: Wind thread forward to front of the beads and tie in the wing segments. Wing should be no longer than the hook length.
Step 4: Whip finish head and place a BB size bead of silicone in front of the beads. Round the silicone as seen on the finished fly and add the stick-on eyes. Let the silicone cure for 12 hours to complete Fred's Alevin.

Whitefish

While the Rocky Mountain whitefish is a nuisance in many Western rivers, they are targeted in some Northwest waters by winter anglers. When the winter water temperatures drop, whitefish school. They can be found in pools or slow flats. On sunny days, the schools can often be seen as the sun reflects off of their shiny bodies as they turn in the current to intercept insects.

If you locate a school of whitefish, nearly any dead-drifted pattern will produce some hot-and-heavy action. A nuisance to the trout fly fisher? Possibly, but try a few from the smokehouse.

Caddis Larva

Whitefish will feed on nearly any small food item that passes their way. One of those foods that they see is the caddis larvae. It is simple to tie, and when nymphed along the bottom produces plenty of action.

Hook: Daiichi 1710, size 12 or 14
Body: Tan Antron, Furry Foam, or your favorite dubbing
Head: Black ostrich herl

Tying Steps
Step 1: Dub or wind on a body of your favorite material.
Step 2: Wind a black ostrich herl

three or four turns to form the head, whip finish and cement to complete the Caddis Larvae.

Simple Whitefish Fly

When I was a kid, this was the only "whitefish" fly available. I used to tie this pattern for the local sporting goods store. Some of the local anglers would tip the fly with a maggot, but that's not necessary. This fly doesn't really resemble any natural food item, but it sure catches whitefish. Tie it in a variety of colors, and fish it right on the bottom.

Hook: Daiichi 1560, size 12 or 14
Thread: Yellow (match body color)
Body: Yellow floss (or virtually any color)
Hackle: Brown neck hackle

Tying Steps
Step 1: Tie in a piece of floss and a neck hackle by the tip.
Step 2: Wind floss forward and secure. Wind hackle forward and

secure. Finish head and cement to complete the Simple Whitefish Fly.

Fuz Ball Egg

Fuz Balls are available at fly shops, or you can go to your local sporting goods store and buy eggs for steelheading, place a drop of Super Glue on your hook and slide the egg on. You now have a very good whitefish fly, as well as trout, Dolly Varden, grayling and steelhead pattern under the right conditions!

Hook: Daiichi 1510, size 12 or 14
Egg: Fuz Ball

Shad

I would venture to say that shad are one of the most overlooked species of fish in the Northwest. Sure, there are a handful of faithful followers who target the shad each season when they return to a few of our rivers, but in comparison to other more glamorous species, the shad has a small following.

Pound for pound, the shad is a powerful fish. Nicknamed "the poor man's steelhead" these herring-like fish battle like there is no tomorrow. On a 6- or 7-weight fly rod they are a most worthy opponent.

There are a few Northwest rivers where shad make an appearance in a big way. The Columbia River in Washington and the Umpqua River in Oregon are two that come to mind. Most of my shad fishing is done in the Columbia.

The last week in May or the first week in June is when all the action usually starts on the Columbia below Bonneville Dam. I usually watch the local newspapers for the fish-ladder count below Bonneville. When the count reaches 30,000 shad per day, I make my move. During the peak of the run that figure can triple.

Shad like current. When fishing below dams on the Columbia, positioning yourself so your fly drifts in the flow will assure you are in the fish zone. Likewise on other rivers. If you can find a rapids, fishing just below will often find schools of fish.

As a rule, sinking lines and sinking flies are a must in order to get down to the shad's level. I often find that a Teeny 200 is about right for the waters I fish most.

Shad Minnow

Small, white and getting down to the fish is what it takes to catch shad. This fly certainly does all of that.

Hook: Daiichi 2220, sizes 12 or 14
Body: Pearl Braid Ribbon
Wing: White marabou
Eyes: Painted lead

Tying Steps
Step 1: Wind on a body of Pearl Braid Ribbon.
Step 2: Tie in the lead eyes using a figure-eight motion of the tying thread.

Step 3: Secure a marabou wing behind the eyes and whip finish.
Step 4: Paint the eyes with acrylic paint as shown to complete the Shad Minnow.

Shad Darter

Another simple, yet effective shad pattern is the Shad Darter. Try this fly in a variety of colors. Remember to fish it on a sinking line or place a split shot on your leader.

Hook: Daiichi 1720, sizes 12 or 14
Thread: Black
Body: Chenille (red, chartreuse and white are my favorites)
Hackle: Match body color

Eyes: Painted on with acrylic or fabric paint

Tying Steps
Step 1: Tie in a piece of chenille and a hen hackle by the tip.

Step 2: Wind the body forward and then the hackle.
Step 3: Whip finish head and cement. When dry, paint on the eyes. When dry, cement again to finish the Shad Darter.

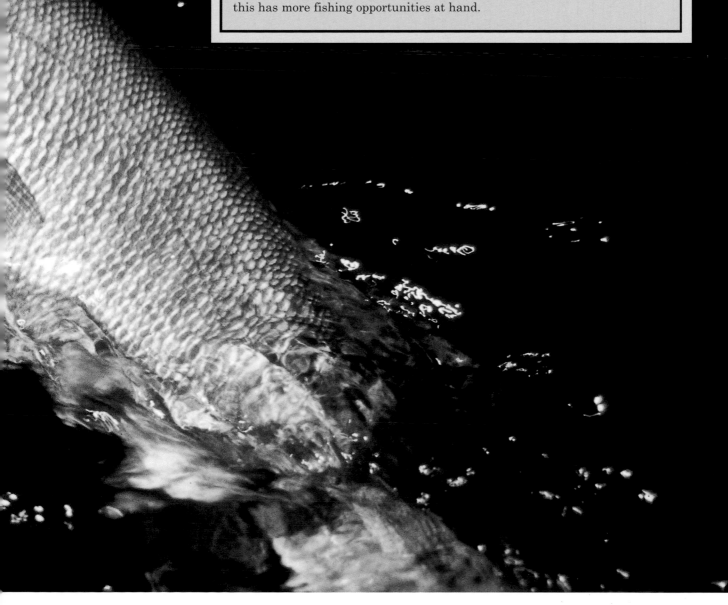

Bass & Panfish

When many people think of bass fishing, visions of Saturday morning TV comes to mind. Glittery boats racing off at 70 mph, bassin' boys chucking various contraptions into the weeds and cranking back a hawg in five seconds flat, only to yell, "yee-haa, boy that was fun" and do it all again. Not real appealing to a fur-and-feather tosser. But bass fishing doesn't have to be that way.

When bass are approached with the fly rod they are great sport. It is big-time excitement to toss a popper into the weeds and have a largemouth pounce on it the second it touches down. Largemouth bass are powerful fighters.

Also it's pretty hard not to like floating a smallmouth stream and having a 100-fish day. Pound for pound smallmouth are pretty tough critters.

Scaling down your equipment will not only make panfish fun, but their abundance often makes for some pretty fast action. A 3-weight rod and a school of crappies is a good way to spend any evening.

Although bass and panfish take a back seat to many of the more glamorous Northwest species, they are certainly deserving of more attention. The Northwest has plenty of water hosting these species, and the fly angler keen to this has more fishing opportunities at hand.

Purple Rabbit Worm

One of the best and most widely used bass baits is the plastic worm. This fly has all the fish-exciting qualities of the plastic worm, and a little more. It has more movement, a little more flash, and when worked through the water properly will catch just as many fish as its crankin' counterpart.

Try this Rabbit Worm in a variety of colors, you never know what color will turn the bass on. My favorites are purple, brown, black, chartreuse and red. Also, when fishing in weedy water you might want to tie this pattern with a monofilament weed guard.

Hook: Daiichi 2441, sizes 2/0-2
Thread: Pink

Tail: Purple rabbit strip, purple Super Floss, purple Holographic Flash
Body: Purple chenille
Hackle: Purple saddle
Eyes: Brass, with an adhesive center

Step 1: Tie in the rabbit strip tail 1 1/2 times the length of the hook shank. Next tie in 2 strands of Super Floss and 2 strands of Holographic Flash on each side of the tail. Trim to length of rabbit strip.

Step 2: Secure the brass eyes.

Step 3: Tie in a piece of purple chenille and a purple saddle hackle by the tip.

Step 4: Wind chenille forward and secure.

Step 5: Wind hackle forward, secure, finish head and cement to complete the Purple Rabbit Worm.

Ole' Rubber Legs

This fly has the main thing that turns a bass on—movement, and plenty of it. When this thing is worked through the water it just looks alive. The rabbit strip and rubber legs flutter and pulsate as the lead eyes give it a jigging action. What self-respecting bass could refuse?

Tie this pattern in a variety of colors and try using any lifelike materials you can think of to add action.

Hook: Daiichi 2720, sizes 5/0-1/0
Thread: Black
Tail: Dyed rabbit strip
Legs: Plastic skirt material
Eyes: Lead, painted
Weed guard: 40-pound monofilament

Tying Steps
Step 1: Cut a piece of 40-pound-test monofilament and secure 1/2 way down the hook shank with your tying thread.
Step 2: Tie in a piece of rabbit strip and several strands of plastic skirt material for the tail.
Step 3: Wind on a body of rabbit strip. Tie in more plastic skirt material 3/4 the way up the hook shank and finish winding rabbit strip forward.
Step 4: Secure the eyes and paint with acrylic or fabric paint.
Step 5: Pull the monofilament forward sliding up through the eye of the hook forming the weed guard. Finish head and cement. Once secured, clip or burn the mono in the eye to complete Ole' Rubber Legs.

Brown Eel

Here is another subsurface bass pattern that gets plenty of attention from ole' bucketmouth as well as from smallmouth bass. This thing just looks alive, and like something good to eat. Fish it around and through the weeds slowly. It's a great fly when the action is slow. Tie it in a variety of colors and sizes. You can just never tell what will turn a bass on.

Hook: Daiichi 2720, sizes 5/0-2
Thread: Orange
Tail: Four black saddle hackles
Body: Brown Leech Yarn
Hackle: Black saddle
Eyes: Bead chain
Weed guard: 40-pound monofilament

Tying Steps
Step 1: Tie in the monofilament to be used for the weed guard 1/2 way down the hooks bend.
Step 2: Secure 4 saddle hackles for the tail.
Step 3: Tie in a piece of Leech Yarn and a saddle hackle by the tip. Wind the yarn forward 3/4 up the hook shank and secure. Wind the hackle forward.
Step 4: Pull the monofilament forward and secure forming the weed guard.
Step 5: Tie in the bead-chain eyes using a figure-eight motion of the tying thread.
Step 6: Tie in more Leech Yarn and taper slightly larger towards the head. Finish head and cement to complete the Brown Eel.

Baby Yellow Perch

Baby yellow perch are a favorite food of bass. Where there are small yellow perch swimming around, bass are sure to be found close by. Swim this fly erratically to mimic the panicky movements of a fleeing baitfish.

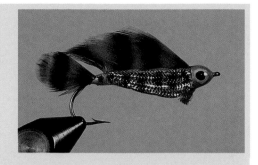

Hook: MI Minnow Body (minnow shape pre-molded to hook), size 4, or standard streamer hook with lead tape or plastic minnow body tied to it.
Thread: Orange monocord
Body: Gold tubular tinsel or Mylar
Tail: 2 olive Chickabou/soft-hackle feathers

Eyes: Painted on with fabric paint
Gills: Red SLF hanks

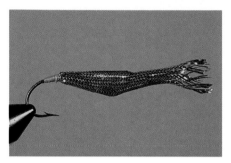

Step 1: Secure tubular tinsel over the underbody as show.

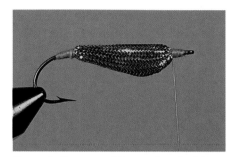

Step 2: Secure tubing at head of fly.

Step 3: Tie in two dark olive soft-hackle feathers.

Step 4: Strip fibers from the quills so the feathers will lie flat along the top of the tubing. Strip fibers only to the length of the body as shown.

Step 5: Place a bead of Super Glue along the top of the tinsel and pull feathers flat against the top of the body. Secure at the butt of the fly with tying thread.

Step 6: Tie in a small tuft of red SLF for the gills, wind on a generous head, tapering into the body and place vertical black bands on the body using a permanent marker.

Step 7: Paint on eyes and cement all thread.

Step 8: Lightly coat the body and head with 5-minute epoxy and turn until set to complete the Baby Yellow Perch.

Panfish Streamer

Panfish, like bass, and most other fish for that matter, will eat smaller fish also. If it will fit in their mouth, any baitfish is in great peril.

Baitfish patterns for panfish need not be fancy. Most hair or marabou streamers will work fine. Here is my favorite.

Hook: Daiichi 2461, sizes 2-6
Thread: Brown
Tail: Brown calf tail
Body: Gold braid, tinsel or Mylar
Underwing: Brown calf tail
Overwing: Yellow marabou

Beard: Red marabou

Tying Steps
Step 1: Tie in a short tail of calf tail.
Step 2: Wind on a body of braid, tinsel or Mylar.

Step 3: Secure an underwing of calf-tail then an overwing of marabou.
Step 4: Tie in a short beard of red marabou, finish head and cement to complete the Panfish Streamer.

Foam Spider

There is something about a spider kicking around on the surface that sends bass and panfish into a tizzy. This foam spider with the long rubber legs does the same.

Hook: Daiichi 1280, sizes 6-10
Thread: Black
Body: Precut foam
Legs: Black tubular rubber legs

Tying Steps
Step 1: Attach thread to hook and tie in rubber legs so that they dangle as shown in the finished fly.

Step 2: Tie in the foam, securing in segments as shown on the finished fly. Whip finish and cement to complete the Foam Spider.

Bug-Eye Bugger

This is a great fly for both smallmouth bass and panfish. Its weight makes it great for vertical fishing around structure. Try it in several colors and sizes.

Hook: Daiichi 1530, sizes 4-10
Thread: Olive
Eyes: Bar-Bell pre-painted
Tail: Black marabou and black rubber leg material
Body: Olive Krystal Chenille
Hackle: Black saddle

Tying Steps
Step 1: Tie in a short tail of black marabou and rubber leg material.
Step 2: Secure a pair of eyes using a figure-eight motion of the tying thread.
Step 3: Secure a piece of olive Krystal

Flash and black saddle hackle by the tip.
Step 4: Wind body material forward, then wind hackle forward and secure behind the eyes. Whip finish and cement to complete the Bug-Eye Bugger.

Foam Popper

Like the Hair Popper, the Foam Popper is big-time fun when bass are feeding on the surface. Poppers are a safe bet during the early morning or late evening hours. Try this popper in several color combinations.

Hook: Daiichi 2720, sizes 5/0-1/0
Thread: Black monocord
Tail: Marabou
Body: Round foam
Legs: Super Floss
Eyes: Doll eyes
Foam coating: Plastic tool-handle dip

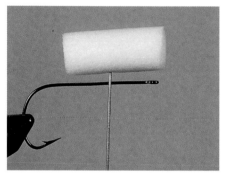

Step 1: Cut a piece of round foam to length as shown.

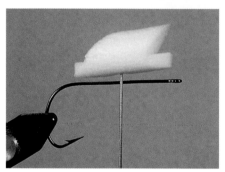

Step 2: Cut the foam as shown in preparation for tying to the hook.

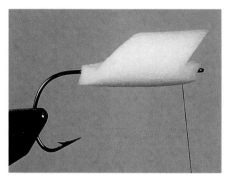

Step 3: Make a small incision on the bottom side of the foam so it sits over the hook shank.

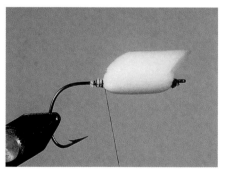

Step 4: Secure foam to the hook front and back with the foam tabs you cut into the foam in Step 2.

Step 5: Tie in a marabou tail.

Step 6: Secure a large clump of Super Floss or rubber hackle in front of the tail using a figure-eight motion of the tying thread.

Step 7: Pulling tail back, dip the entire body in the plastic tool handle dip and hang to dry.

Step 8: Glue on plastic doll eyes and clean out the eye of the hook to complete the Foam Popper.

Hair Popper

When bass are willing to take topwater flies there is nothing more fun than throwing poppers at them. The water literally explodes when a largemouth bass sucks a big bug from the surface.

Hair poppers can be tied in virtually any color combination. Tie some with monofilament weed guards for those times when fishing in the weeds is required.

Hook: Daiichi 2720, sizes 5/0-1/0
Thread: Black
Tail: Four soft-hackle feathers (match body color), and several strands of Super Floss
Skirt: A hackle to match tail feathers

Body: Deer body hair
Legs: Super Floss or rubber hackle
Eyes: Doll eyes

Step 1: Tie in a tail of four matched, wide soft-hackle feathers with convex sides together. Also tie in Super Floss as shown.

Step 2: Tie in two more hackles to match the tail feathers and wind several turns. Fold this skirt towards the back of the fly and pin down with your tying thread.

Step 3: Select a clump of deer hair and begin spinning it in place. Pin some of the hair ends back, adding to the skirt.

Step 4: Keep spinning clumps of deer hair forward, packing tightly. 2/3 the way up the hook tie in more Super Floss for the legs.

Step 5: Continue spinning and packing deer hair forward to the eye of the hook.

Step 6: With sharp scissors trim hair into the popper shape. Trim Super Floss legs to even lengths.

Step 7: Glue doll eyes in place with 5-minute epoxy to complete the Hair Popper.

Baby Bass

The baby bass is in danger, just like any small fish, whenever larger forage fish are present. I find this pattern especially effective for bass when erratically stripped around structure.

Hook: Mustad 34011 or equivalent, size 2
Thread: Monofilament
Tail: Olive and black marabou
Body: Orvis E-Z Braid Body colored with permanent markers
Eyes: painted with fabric paint

Step 1: Tie in a tail of mixed olive and black marabou.

Step 2: Secure a piece of Orvis E-Z Braid Body at the butt of the fly.

Step 3: Secure the body at the head without pulling tight (makes for a fatter body), trim excess and form a large, tapered head with the monofilament.

Step 4: Color the E-Z Braid with permanent markers to look like a baby bass. I use green and black for the back, then red for the gills.

Step 5: Paint on eyes as shown.

Step 6: Coat the body with 5-minute epoxy and turn until set to complete the Baby Bass.

Bass Bunny

A favorite largemouth bass pattern by Jon Luke, the Bass Bunny is a killer fly when bass are feeding on their smaller brethren. Fish the Bass Bunny by retrieving it with short, erratic strips, followed by a two- or three-second pause. This mimics the way a baby bass moves through structure. The pauses trigger explosive strikes when fished shallow, over wood or vegetation.

Hook: 6X long streamer hook, sizes 1-4

Thread: White 6/0

Body: Lead wire, flat Diamond Braid, dark olive rabbit strip, and white rabbit strip connected with Dave's Flexament and Zap-A-Gap

Lateral line and gills: Black Flashabou, clear Krystal Flash, and red Krystal Flash

Head cement: Griff's Pearl

Tying Steps

Step 1: Cover the hook shank with thread and add several turns of lead wire. Secure a piece of Diamond Braid at the butt.

Step 2: Wrap the Diamond Braid up the shank and secure near the eye.

Step 3: Punch the hook point through the white rabbit strip about 0.25 inch from the butt. Apply a couple of drops of Super Glue inside the rabbit strip, pull it forward, and tie it down behind the eye of the hook.

Step 4: Tie in the olive rabbit strip to the top of the hook behind the eye. Apply some Dave's Flexament on the tag piece of white rabbit and Super Glue along the top of the hook shank. Attach the olive rabbit strip to the Diamond Braid by pulling back and finally connecting the tags of the white and olive rabbit with Dave's Flexament.

Step 5: Tie in several strands of black Flashabou and clear Krystal Flash so they lay down the lateral line for the length of the fly. For the gills, tie in a pinch of red Krystal Flash, trim it to 0.5 inch, and whip finish.

Step 6: Apply a drop or two of Super Glue and set the eyes just behind the hook eye over the Krystal Flash and Flashabou.

Bottomfish

Fly fishing for bottomfish is not widely practiced in the Northwest, but is possible under certain conditions. Not all bottom feeders are found only on the bottom all the time. In fact, there are times when certain species can be found right on the surface.

The species most often targeted are black rockfish, surfperch and lingcod. All of these fish can be taken in shallow water, putting them in range of the fly fisher. I have even taken halibut on the fly, but conditions need to be just right for this to happen.

Jetties, reefs and kelp beds are excellent places to start looking for rockfish and lingcod. These areas are not hard to find along the Pacific coast and, if you have access to a sea-worthy boat the possibilities are endless.

One consistency with the bottom feeders is that they are not real picky feeders. Being opportunistic eaters, they will attack nearly anything that passes their way that looks like food. Specific fly patterns imitating their natural foods are usually not required. If your fly has movement, it will probably work.

Halfarabbit

Most often when I am fishing the depths of the ocean, or over rock piles, or in the kelp beds, I use my Halfarabbit fly. It doesn't matter if I am fishing for rockfish, lingcod or halibut—the Halfarabbit is my first choice.

The bottom species are not overly picky feeders. They will attack nearly anything that moves. There are exceptions to this, of course, but generally speaking, if it moves, it's food.

The Halfarabbit certainly moves, it's durable and has taken a lot of bottomfish for

me. Tie this fly in a variety of sizes and colors for virtually every bottomfish species.

Hook: Daiichi 2546 or similar stainless saltwater hook, sizes 6/0-1/0
Thread: Chartreuse
Tail: Dyed rabbit strip, fluorescent Flashabou, Krystal Flash
Underbody: Large lead wire

Body: Dyed rabbit strip

Tying Steps
Step 1: Cover the hook shank with large lead wire.
Step 2: Depending on the size of fly, tie in from two to six strips of rabbit

strip for the tail. Next tie in a hefty bunch of fluorescent Flashabou and then Krystal Flash over that.
Step 3: Cover the entire hook shank by winding with rabbit strip.
Step 4: Finish head and cement to complete the Halfarabbit.

Purple Worm

Like the Halfarabbit, this fly had plenty of movement. Tie it in several colors because...you never know! I use this pattern mostly for rockfish and lingcod.

Hook: Daiichi 2546, sizes 4/0-2/0
Thread: Black monocord
Tail: Dyed rabbit strip
Body: Dyed rabbit strip
Eyes: Bar-Bell pre-painted.

Tying Steps
Step 1: Tie in a tail of dyed rabbit strip.
Step 2: Wind on a body of dyed rabbit strip.

Step 3: Tie in Bar-Bell eyes, finish head and cement to complete the Purple Worm.

Perch Bugger

The Woolly Bugger is not only good for most freshwater species, it is also good for many saltwater species. I tie this Bugger on a heavy saltwater hook, and it is my favorite tie for surfperch when fishing off jetties or along the Pacific beaches. Try it in orange, red and yellow.

Hook: Daiichi 2546, size 6
Thread: Black or orange
Tail: Orange marabou and orange Krystal Flash
Body: Orange chenille
Hackle: Grizzly

Option: Tie in some lead eyes when fishing this pattern in deeper water

Tying Steps
Step 1: Tie in a tail of marabou and Krystal Flash.

Step 2: Tie in a grizzly hackle by the tip and a piece of chenille.
Step 3: Wind chenille forward, then wind hackle forward.
Step 4: Finish head and cement to complete the Perch Bugger.

Fluorescent Flashabou Shrimp

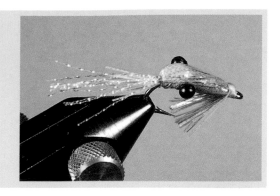

Shrimp are a favorite food item for many saltwater species. Although most bottomfish are not real snooty about the food they eat, using imitations of a natural food is always best. This shrimp is an easy-to-tie pattern that imitates a common food item here in the Northwest.

During low-light situations such as late evening, this is a great shrimp imitation because it is tied with fluorescent materials. It can be illuminated with a flashlight or strobe, possibly giving the angler a real advantage.

Hook: Daiichi 2546, size 4
Antennae: Pink Krystal Flash
Body/shellback/throat: Pink fluorescent Flashabou
Eyes: Mono eyes

Tying Steps
Step 1: Tie in several strands of pink Krystal Flash at the bend of the hook.

Step 2: Secure the Mono Eyes directly above the hook point.
Step 3: Tie in a bunch of Flashabou and leave pointing past the bend of the hook with the antennae to be used later for a shellback.
Step 4: Tie in more Flashabou and wind towards the eye of the hook and secure.
Step 5: Pull Flashabou from Step 3

over the top of the shrimp body and secure at the eye forming the shellback. Leave several strands facing to the rear and clip to the length as shown in the finished fly. Fold remaining Flashabou under the eye and tie down as a throat. Clip to the length of the hook gape, finish head and cement to complete the Fluorescent Flashabou Shrimp.

Saltwater Minnow

Among the most common forage foods for most bottom species is other fish. This minnow is hard to beat when the baitfish are on the small size.

Hook: Daiichi 2546, size 2
Thread: Monofilament
Tail: Olive marabou

Body: Orvis E-Z Braid
Eyes: Painted on with fabric paint
Body markings: Permanent markers

Tying Steps
See instructions for the Baby Bass, page 80.

Psychedelic Squid

This fly is simply a material combination tied for flash and movement. I suppose it could resemble the general appearance of a squid, but I'm sure the rockfish I have caught with it simply take it because it is there—in front of their face! I have tried a plethora of color and material combinations in the tying of this fly.

Hook: Daiichi 2546, size 2/0
Thread: Red
Tail: Combination of various saddle hackles, and synthetic wing materials
Hackle: Grizzly (any color will do)
Body: Tying thread
Eyes: Gold bead chain

Tying Steps
Step 1: Tie in a bunch of synthetic wing materials (SLF, Super Hair, FisHair, etc.) so they extend the length of the hook shank past the bend.
Step 2: Secure two or four pairs of saddle hackles so they extend slightly

past the synthetics.
Step 3: Wind two or three saddle hackles in front of the tails.
Step 4: Tie in bead eyes and taper a body with the tying thread back to the hackle as seen on the finished fly. Cement thread to complete the Psychedelic Squid.

Carp

There are probably more carp in Northwest waters than any other species of fish. There are probably fewer carp anglers than there are anglers for any other species. Heads turn when you talk about carpin' with a fly. Most people get a sick look on their face and inquire why anyone in their right mind would want to fish for carp? The answer is really very simple. Carp are incredible fighters, and extremely difficult to get interested in an artificial fly. When hooked, their fight is ferocious.

I would venture to say that carp are the most challenging species we have in Northwest waters. They are smart, extremely nervous fish that spook incredibly easily. Rarely is a carp taken by blind casting. Accurate, long casts are almost always required.

The secret to success when fly rodding for carp is concentration. Observe fish that are slowly feeding along the bottom in shallow water such as small bays off rivers or in shallow shorelines around lakes. Delicately place your fly a few feet in front of a feeding fish, and if your cast doesn't spook it, watch carefully. When the carp gets close to where you think your fly should be, set the hook at any movement of the fish—head turn, direction change, tail rising, etc. Ninety-nine percent of the time you will not feel the fish unless you set the hook. Carp suck your fly in and spit it out again faster than you can say dang! They are a most humbling fish.

Carp fishing may not be for everyone, but they certainly become an addiction for anyone that tries it, and is successful. They are a most worthy opponent, and best of all, we don't seem to be running out of them!

Jon's Carp Bug

This is a fly designed by Jon Luke, a friend, and total carp addict. Experimenting with several ties, this is Jon's favorite pattern when fishing the shallows for carp. The long hackle makes this fly very seductive when twitched in front of a feeding fish.

Hook: Daiichi 2151, size 4
Thread: Black
Body: Black dubbing
Hackle: Red-brown saddle
Shellback: Lacquered turkey quill

Tying Steps
Step 1: Tie in a stiff saddle hackle by the tip, and a section of turkey quill.
Step 2: Dub on a body using your favorite dubbing.
Step 3: Wind hackle forward working the fibers to the sides of the fly as shown.
Step 4: Pull turkey quill forward and secure at head. Whip finish head, and cement or lacquer the entire shellback and head to complete Jon's Carp Bug.

Carpin' Dad

Carp will feed on almost any available food at times. Small crayfish are certain targets at times. This is a simple fly that works well when fished over rocky areas where both crayfish and carp are found. Cast out and let the fly sit motionless until a carp is within range. Give the fly a few quick, short strips—and hold on!

Hook: Daiichi 2220, size 6
Thread: Rust
Antenna: 2 strands of copper Flashabou
Body: Copper or rust-colored Leech Yarn or dubbing
Legs: Brown hackle
Eyes: Mono eyes
Shellback: Copper Swiss straw
Rib: Copper wire

Tying Steps
Step 1: Tie in 2 strands of Flashabou for the antennae.
Step 2: Secure the mono eyes.
Step 3: Tie in the body material and wind to behind the eyes.
Step 4: Secure a piece of copper wire and a saddle hackle by the tip behind the eyes.
Step 5: Wind the body .25 inch and secure. Wind the hackle .25 inch and secure. Now finish winding the body to the eye and secure.
Step 6: With the copper wire, secure a piece of Swiss straw behind the eyes with 2 turns, and then wind the wire to the eye of the hook, creating a segmented body. Trim Swiss straw to length as seen in the finished fly. Whip finish and cement to complete the Carpin' Dad.

Carp Woolly

This is a simple fly with plenty of movement. When twitched in front of a feeding carp it often does the trick.

Hook: Daiichi 1720, size 8
Thread: Black
Underbody: Lead-free wire
Body: Black chenille
Hackle: Grizzly dry-fly hackle

Tying Steps
Step 1: Wind lead-free wire up the hook shank and secure with tying thread.
Step 2: Tie in a piece of black chenille and a grizzly hackle by the tip.
Step 3: Wind the hackle forward and secure. Finish head and cement to complete the Carp Woolly.

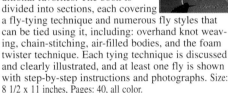

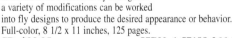